The Ten Commandments

. . . are no longer relevant today!
. . . are for the Jews only!
. . . are an archaic legal code!

And so go many excuses. This book presents the Decalogue as the very Word of God to all people everywhere in all ages. You don't earn salvation by keeping the Ten Commandments, but you certainly follow them as a Christian committed to the Lord Jesus Christ.

THE AUTHOR / Leslie B. Flynn has pastored the Grace Conservative Baptist Church of Nanuet, New York since 1949. He is a graduate of Moody Bible Institute (pastor's course), Wheaton College (B.A.), Eastern Baptist Theological Seminary (B.D.), the University of Pennsylvania (M.A. in philosophy), and received a D.D. from Conservative Baptist Theological Seminary of Denver in 1963. He has been an instructor in journalism at Nyack Missionary College and has long been active as an author. His other books under the Victor label include *Me Be Like Jesus?,* a study in Christlike living, and *19 Gifts of the Spirit,* an in-depth study of the spiritual gifts.

Now a Word from Our Creator

Leslie B. Flynn

While this book is designed for the reader's personal use and profit, it is also intended for group study. A leader's guide is available from your local bookstore or from the publisher at 95¢.

VICTOR BOOKS
a division of SP Publications, Inc.

All quotations in this book are used by permission of the copyright holders, and are noted in connection with each particular quotation. To these copyright holders we express our thanks. In addition, we want to credit the following:

"The Source of Law and Justice," by Howard E. Kershner, reprinted by permission from *Applied Christianity,* July 1972, 7960 Crescent Avenue, Buena Park, CA 90620; "What Code of Values Can We Teach Our Children?" by William V. Shannon, *New York Times Magazine,* January 16, 1972, © 1972 by The New York Times Company; reprinted by permission; as condensed in May 1972 *Reader's Digest; God Speaks to an X-rated Society,* edited by Alan F. Johnson, copyright 1973, Moody Press, Moody Bible Institute of Chicago; used by permission.

Library of Congress Catalog Card Number: 75–36901
ISBN: 0-88207-728-7

VICTOR BOOKS
A division of SP Publications, Inc.
P. O. Box 1825 ● Wheaton, Ill. 60187

Contents

To my secretaries through the years:
  Mrs. Dorothea Rasmussen
  Mrs. Barbara Jacobsen Ibarra
  Mrs. Sandra Nicholson
for their patient, valuable, and faithful services.

Preface

Recently a TV documentary spent an hour describing the many types of rip-offs in modern dishonest business practices which cost the American public millions of dollars annually. In his closing remarks the commentator asked, "Who is going to teach ethics to the next generation?"

As part of its message, the church teaches the Ten Commandments, which furnish an objective standard of right and wrong in short propositional form as fixed rules of life.

When the Israelites were about to enter the Promised Land, God reminded the new generation of these laws. Obeying the commandments would bring blessing, but disobedience would mean disaster, both individually and nationally.

As Billy Graham said at a recent National Prayer Breakfast, "We may not survive unless there is a spiritual revival." We need to hear the voice of God calling us back to the principles of morality enunciated in the Decalogue. We need to rescue, repeat, and reemphasize the Ten Commandments.

This applies to all lands, for "righteousness exalteth a nation, but sin is a reproach to any people" (Prov. 14:34).

A Child's Ten Commandments

I   Thou no gods shalt have but Me

II   Before no idol bend the knee

III   Take not the name of God in vain

IV   Dare not the Sabbath to profane

V   Give both thy parents honor due

VI   Take heed that thou no murder do

VII   Abstain from all that is unclean

VIII   Steal not though thou be poor or mean

IX   Make not a willful lie nor love it

X   What is thy neighbor's do not covet.

—Author unknown

Introduction

Principles of Interpretation

In order for the Ten Commandments to be correctly understood and applied to daily life, certain principles of interpretation are needed. These can be summarized as six basic rules.

Rule 1 *Prohibitions include opposite positive commands. Positive commands involve contrary negative duties.*

A newspaper editor gave an applicant for a rewrite job the assignment of rewriting the Ten Commandments. He turned in a sheet of paper with one word written on it: "Don't."

However, the eight commandments stated negatively could be rewritten with a "Do." For instance, "Thou shalt not take the name of the Lord thy God in vain" can be rendered, "Thou shalt hallow the name of the Lord thy God." And "Thou shalt not kill" can be rephrased, "Thou shalt honor the sanctity of human life."

Likewise, the two commands worded positively include the prohibition of contrary expressions. "Honor thy father and thy mother" can be restated, "Thou shalt not disobey thy parents."

A few minutes' deliberation should enable anyone to reword all 10 rules in both positive and negative fashion.

Rule 2 *Commands extend to thought life.*

Any precept that forbids an outward act also prohibits the mental pursuit of that act. Christ illustrated this principle in the Sermon on the Mount on two commands, the sixth and seventh. He pointed out that the command against murder is broken by hateful thoughts or knifing words, both of which are potential murder (Matt. 5:21-22). He also declared that the command against adultery is broken by lustful thinking, which is mental adultery (Matt. 5:27-28).

Rule 3 *Every inducement which leads to a transgression of a commandment is also forbidden.*

When an act is expressly forbidden, anything that would lead to that act is likewise included in the prohibition. Some sins, though not expressly forbidden in the Decalogue, are conducive to the breaking of one or more of the commandments, and are thereby forbidden in every command to whose violation they contribute.

An example is drunkenness. Ezekiel Hopkins, a 17th-century Anglican bishop, pointed out that though drunkenness is not mentioned in the Ten Commandments, it is, in principle, forbidden several times over because it encourages the transgression of several commands. How much easier to blaspheme, steal, lie, or kill, when intoxicated. Every command subverted by intoxication implicitly forbids drunkenness. This principle of interpretation becomes very significant in view of the estimate that 14% of high school seniors across the U.S. get drunk at least once a week (Enid Nemy, "Youth's Alcohol Abuse Called 'Alarming' Here," *New York Times,* Aug. 19, 1974).

Rule 4 *Each command forbids sins of a similar nature. Hence, each command presents a specific case of a more general rule, usually the worst possible breach.*

When the Decalogue says, "Thou shalt not kill," does it permit half-killing someone? On the contrary, the sixth commandment not only forbids murder but also condemns all cruelty and injury to human life short of murder. The command requires every care and consideration to alleviate the sufferings of humanity. But the command is formulated to present not only a specific case of a more general command, but the worst possible crime against human personality—murder.

11

The command "Thou shalt not bear false witness" rules out not only lying and perjury but all sister sins such as slander, flattery, and gross exaggeration.

"Honor thy father and thy mother" is a specific example of a more general command, "Honor authority." Perhaps obedience to parents is singled out because parental authority is the first rule a child meets in life and yielding to parents prepares the child for authorities he will meet later: teachers, employers, and God.

Rule 5 *The Ten Commandments may be summed up under two. In general, the first division is more important than the second.*

The first four commands relate to our duties toward God; the last six, to our duties toward our fellow men. Perhaps when the law was originally written on two tables of stone, our duties to God were inscribed on one table, our obligations to our neighbor on the other. At any rate, the ten readily reduce to two: love to God, and love to neighbor. Love is the common denominator of these two summations. "The end of the commandment is charity [love] out of a pure heart" (1 Tim. 1:5).

Today we hear about neighbor-love. Situation ethics says, in effect, "Let love be your guide." But nebulous, vague, ethereal "love," influenced by the depravity and deceit of the human heart, needs guidelines in order to make decisions that are truly loving. So the commandments provide markers to indicate the course of true neighbor-love. Genuine love does not commit adultery, no matter how meaningful a relationship may be. Love does not steal another's possessions, nor spoil another's reputation. As Paul put it, "Love is the fulfilling of the law" (Rom. 13:10).

Jesus commented on the two-fold division of the Ten Commandments when He answered a lawyer's question as to which is the great commandment in the law (Matt. 22:37-40). Love to God is the first and great commandment. And the second is like unto it—love to neighbor. In general, love to God takes priority over love to man. Let no one think that by fulfilling his obligations to his neighbor he has done his complete duty. Unless he has loved God with all his heart, soul, mind, and body, he is guilty of breaking the first and great commandment.

Rule 6 To break one is to be guilty of all.

A final principle reminds us that the commands are so closely related that to break one is to be under judgment for all. The same Authority which forbids murder forbids stealing and lying. To disobey the Authority at one point is to disobey the Authority which stands behind all. "Whosoever shall keep the whole law, and yet offend in one point, he is guilty of all" (James 2:10).

The Ten Commandments

(Exodus 20:3-17)

ONE: Thou shalt have no other gods before Me.

TWO: Thou shalt not make unto thee any graven image, or any likeness of anything that is in heaven above, or that is in the earth beneath, or that is in the water under the earth; thou shalt not bow down thyself to them, nor serve them; for I the Lord thy God am a jealous God, visiting the iniquity of the fathers upon the children unto the third and fourth generation of them that hate Me; and showing mercy unto thousands of them that love Me and keep My commandments.

THREE: Thou shalt not take the name of the Lord thy God in vain; for the Lord will not hold him guiltless that taketh His name in vain.

FOUR: Remember the Sabbath Day, to keep it holy. Six days shalt thou labor and do all thy work; but the seventh day is the sabbath of the Lord thy God. In it thou shalt not do any work, thou, nor thy son, nor thy daughter, thy manservant, nor thy maidservant, nor thy cattle, nor thy stranger that is within thy gates; for in six days the Lord made heaven and earth, the sea, and all that in them is, and rested the seventh day. Wherefore the Lord blessed the Sabbath Day and hallowed it.

FIVE: Honor thy father and thy mother, that thy days may be long upon the land which the Lord thy God giveth thee.

SIX: Thou shalt not kill.

SEVEN: Thou shalt not commit adultery.

EIGHT: Thou shalt not steal.

NINE: Thou shalt not bear false witness against thy neighbor.

TEN: Thou shalt not covet thy neighbor's house; thou shalt not covet thy neighbor's wife, nor his manservant, nor his maidservant, nor his ox, nor his ass, nor anything that is thy neighbor's.

1

Whatever Happened to
the Ten Commandments?

"He wrote upon the tables . . . the ten commandments" (Ex. 34:28).

A student at a well-known university returned to his apartment from the supermarket. From the inside pockets of his raincoat he unloaded two T-bone steaks and four lamb chops. He had carried them home in this unusual place because he hadn't paid for them. "It doesn't bother me," said the student. "They don't miss it in a big store like that. And besides, they add the losses to the price of everything we buy anyway."

A salesgirl with a master's degree in marketing confided to a friend that she had deliberately soiled a dress so she could mark it down and buy it herself at a bargain price.

When the friend questioned her ethics, she shrugged it off. "You think that's bad! A lot of girls would steal it outright—which isn't very smart. The way I do it, nothing shows up missing." To her, *wrong* was to steal in a stupid or obvious way.

Three-fifths of the senior class of a leading eastern university reportedly lived with a student of the opposite sex without benefit of marriage during the 1973-74 academic year. Their defense: "If yours is a meaningful relationship, a marriage license isn't needed!"

Widespread disrespect for authority, murder, crimes of violence, unchastity, marital infidelity, graft, bribery, stealing, cheating, lying, slander—all proclaim a woeful neglect or abysmal ignorance of the moral law of God known as the Ten Commandments or Decalogue. A national Gallup poll in Canada revealed that one of every ten could not name even one of the Ten Commandments, and one out of three could not name three.

Some people voice blatant opposition to the Decalogue. A professor in a Monday morning sociology class scornfully held up a newspaper clipping reporting a Sunday sermon on the Ten Commandments. "Hopelessly out of date!" he ranted. "The Ten Commandments bind the civilized world to barbarism. They are antisocial, based on superstition."

On the other hand, the church may be somewhat to blame for ignorance in the area of practical morality. A century ago the president of Great Britain's St. Andrews University issued this indictment: "Many a hundred sermons have I heard . . . but never, during these 30 years, never one that I can recollect on common honesty, or these primitive commandments, 'Thou shalt not lie,' and 'Thou shalt not steal' " (J. A. Froude, "Inaugural Address," St. Andrews University, 1869, quoted in *Handbook of Preaching Resources from English Literature,* edited by James Douglas Robertson, Macmillan, N.Y., 1962). Many a church a century later, strong in doctrine, is strangely silent on duty.

Surprisingly, silence on the Decalogue causes little concern in some Christian quarters. In fact, some Christians feel that since we are not under law but under grace it savors of legalism to teach or preach on the Commandments. One pastor advised soft-pedaling them in the presence of children lest little ones think they can earn heaven by keeping them. Another pastor, floundering in confusion as to the place of the law today, wrote in a Christian periodical, "Are we Christian preachers supposed to preach the Ten Commandments?"

One young minister, who had just finished preaching on the Decalogue in his church, was invited to bring a series of studies to a nearby weeknight Bible class. He started on the Ten Commandments, but before long the leaders strongly hinted that he should switch to another study.

Yet Christ Himself said, "Whosoever therefore shall break one of these least commandments, and shall teach men so, he shall be called the least in the kingdom of heaven; but whosoever shall do and teach them, the same shall be called great in the kingdom of heaven" (Matt. 5:19). In the passage immediately following He comments on the sixth and seventh commandments, showing He has the Ten Commandments in mind. Is not neglect of teaching the Commandments thus placed under the censure of Christ?

The Decalogue remains indispensable in the twentieth century because it is

- a resumé of morality
- a restraint on evil
- a revealer of sin
- a regulator of Christian behavior
- a road map to happiness

The Ten Commandments as a Resumé of Morality

Someone commented, "It seems incredible. Man has made 35 million laws and yet hasn't improved on the Ten Commandments."

Mankind needs an objective standard of right and wrong. Conscience is insufficient, for it informs a person only if he is obeying or disobeying standards he has previously accepted, whether or not those standards are correct.

Also, man needs God's moral law stated in short, summarized form. The Ten Commandments furnish such a summary, giving us condensed statements on how to live successfully. The conciseness of their expression, plus the vast scope of their implications, exhibit their divine origin. Only God could have reduced the whole ethical obligation of man to so small a space. These ten rules cover the entire range of man's duty and forbid every type of wrong-doing. The rest of the Bible is, among other things, a commentary on these ten rules, amplifying, interpreting, warning against their violation, as well as giving historical examples of those who have kept or broken them. When one learns the Ten Commandments, he has at his disposal the essence of ethics, the seed-plot of morality, and the kernel of correct conduct in any generation.

In addition to their concise, compact, staccatolike formulation, the Ten Commandments have many other unique characteristics. They were written by the finger of God. They were written on two tables of stone, inscribed on both sides, likely because the material required that much space, though some commentators suggest the same words were written twice, once on the front, the other on the reverse. They were specifically called "the ten commandments" (Ex. 34:28).

This code was first given orally in the hearing of the people who stood on the plain at the base of the colossal pulpit of Mount Sinai. With the mountain smoking and quaking, trumpets blaring and blasting, lightning flashing and thunder crashing, God spoke these 10 words (see Heb. 12:18-21). This spectacular event dramatized the majesty of the Almighty, the awesome character of the law, and the terrifying consequences of its violation. Not surprisingly, the Ten Commandments were placed in the Ark of the Covenant in the Holy of Holies. They were repeated to a new generation about to enter the Promised Land (Deut. 5:1-21).

Though originally given to the Hebrews, the Ten Commandments express God's standard of conduct for all men in all times. Interestingly, the source of law and justice in our western world has been traced to the Ten Commandments. Dr. Howard E. Kershner, former president of the Christian Freedom Foundation and relief administrator who has closely observed the workings of governments in 40 countries, makes this observation. In early British history . . .

> . . . more generally than now, men believed that God created the universe, including man, in accordance with certain very definite principles which have been called the Natural Law or the Moral Law of God. They are well summarized in the Ten Commandments, enlarged by other provisions in the Law of Moses, became the unwritten or Common Law of England. . . . In like manner, the Common Law of Britain was accepted as the basis of our legal system in the United States and in other British colonies. . . . We find, therefore, that the Bible is at the basis of jurisprudence, especially in all English-speaking countries, and to a remarkable, if lesser, degree in all Western countries (Howard E. Kershner, "The Source of Law and Justice," *Applied Christianity*, July 1972).

In his book *The Case for Christianity*, C. S. Lewis affirms that different civilizations have had quite similar moralities. He names several moral principles which have no exceptions. No people anywhere have ever held that running away in a battle should be admired, that double-crossing your closest friend should make you feel proud, that cruelty to children, rape, or taking any woman is right. Contrary to popular belief, moral principles do not differ vastly from culture to culture. In the appendix of *Abolition of Man,* Lewis shows similarities between the moral codes of great civilizations and the neighbor-love of the Decalogue.

Relativism tries to get rid of all absolutes. "Never say 'never,'" the relativist declares, for everything is relative. Yet absolutely sure there are no absolutes, he sets up his own absolutes.

A university professor denied that the Ten Commandments were universally true, arguing all have exceptions. He then proceeded to list two of his own commands which he said Christians had missed: "Be intelligent and be tolerant." A student asked if there were any exceptions to these two. Caught on the horns of a dilemma—should he deny an exception and thus admit his commandments are universal—he paused before answering, "One should be tolerant of everyone *except* those who are not tolerant." The student, not wishing to further embarrass the professor, refrained from asking, "Should we be intelligent *except* with those who are not intelligent?"

Significantly, the professor's added commandment "Be tolerant," is only a variation of the Ten Commandments. The second table of the law, summed up as love to a neighbor, certainly includes tolerance. Paradoxically, those who deny the Ten Commandments often set up their own laws which are hauntingly similar to one or more of the Ten.

The Apostle Paul stated that Gentile nations show "the work of the law written in their hearts" (Rom. 2:15). Fogged by the fall, however, man needs open publication and clarification of this inward law. This needed enlightenment is provided in summary fashion by the pithy pointers of the Decalogue.

The Ten Commandments as a Restraint on Evil

"What did you learn in Sunday School today?" asked Johnny's mother.

"Oh, all about the Ten Commandos," came Johnny's reply.

Perhaps Johnny wasn't so far wrong. An acquaintance with the Ten Commandments may do more to safeguard the future of an individual than the protection of a hundred commandos.

A driver noticed traffic in front of him beginning to slow considerably. Then he spotted the reason. Leading the line was a shiny, black car with long antenna and red light on top, driven by a man in uniform. Yes, the law restrains. When the police car pulled off to the side, most of the cars resumed their previous, slightly excessive speed.

Similarly, a knowledge of the divine moral summary will often serve as a check against breaking it. Though we do not hold with Socrates that knowledge is virtue, nor that teaching the law invariably produces law-keeping people, nevertheless, a knowledge of God's law is bound to restrain some evil. For example, two new boys arrive at a summer camp which is governed by certain rules. By oversight one boy does not receive a copy of the camp regulations. Who will more likely keep the rules, the one who received a copy, or the boy who didn't see them? Likewise, those familiar with God's ethical rules will more likely obey them than those who somehow have not learned them.

Dr. Carl Henry says:

> Even where there is no saving faith, the Law serves to restrain sin and to preserve the order of creation by proclaiming the will of God. . . . It has the role of a magistrate who is a terror to evildoers. By its proclamation that God approves conformity to the law's demands, it provides additional sanctions for rectitude. The Law thus promotes order in the domain of common grace. It fulfills a political function, therefore, by its contrasting influence in the unregenerate world (*Christian Personal Ethics*, Eerdmans, Grand Rapids, Mich.).

One reason for widespread breakdown in moral behavior is that the stern "thou shalts" and "thou shalt nots" with all their personal and social implications do not receive major emphasis in our culture. Those who deal with delinquency often remark about the relationship between crime and lack of ethical instruction. Of 43,000 youths who faced a Tennessee judge over a 20-year period, only 122 were attending Sunday School regularly, where they would have made some acquaintance with the Decalogue.

A cursory examination of the Ten Commandments reveals a few diverse, scattered, unrelated, though specific rules, touching here and there in the field of moral conduct. But an in-depth study of their ramifications shows the all-inclusiveness of this code of behavior. No single command should be regarded as a mere lone order exhaustible by one explanation, but rather as a gate opening into a wide field of conduct, demanding perfection in every hedge and corner of that particular area of ethics.

In its totality the Decalogue forbids every conceivable sin, demands every possible virtue, condemning omissions of duty as well as commissions of misdeeds. It comprises a perfect rule of life which Christ inferred by saying, "This do and thou shalt live" (Luke 10:28). No scriptural maxim of behavior escapes classification under one or more of the ten rules.

In bare outline the Ten Commandments help deter wrong-doing. But when these skeletal statements are fleshed out through application of certain rules of interpretation, the far-reaching implications of the Decalogue become more apparent. (See the *Introduction* for a list and brief explanation of these rules of interpretation.)

Those who understand the implications of the Decalogue through the use of these six rules should be armed with a strong deterrent against committing moral evil. One youth leader said, "If our young people were as well grounded in the meaning and ramifications of the Ten Commandments as they are in reading, writing, and arithmetic, untold suffering, trouble, and sorrow might be averted, and a better generation would grow up."

The Ten Commandments as a Revealer of Sin

"But," object some Christian leaders, "won't stress upon the commandments make people think they can get into heaven by keeping them?"

To the contrary, when the implications of the Ten Commandments are understood, who dares claim perfection of life in thought, word, and deed? Senator Harold Hughes, who left the United States Congress to pursue Christian service, confessed, "Except for premeditated murder, I've broken every one of the Ten Commandments."

In the brilliant spotlight of divine holiness our blots and blemishes loom large, showing us our inability to meet God's standard and making us admit our need for forgiveness. To the conscientious person, rather than give hope for heaven, the Decalogue will bring cause for despair, and create a sense of need for a Redeemer from the penalty which attaches to even the smallest violation. Failure, futility, and frustration weigh down the one whose hope of heaven is based on obedience to the law. Just as a mirror shows a dirty face and drives us to soap and water, the Ten Commandments reflect the uncleanness of our hearts and direct us to the cleansing Christ.

Evangelists maintain that minimal sense of sin in the unconverted is a major obstacle in winning people to Christ. May not a soft-pedaling of the Ten Commandments contribute to this condition? A missionary from Bolivia told how a whole Indian camp had changed—no more stealing, no more immorality. But the missionary also reported this interesting fact. When he started to preach the Gospel, there was no response whatever. The Indians couldn't understand the love of God. So the missionaries decided to drill the Decalogue into them. The result—the Indians saw their guilt before God. The law became their schoolmaster to bring them to Christ (Gal. 3:24).

No person can intelligently receive Christ who has not first had a sense of sin. Since sin is want of conformity to the law of God, by a knowledge of that law comes a sense of sin. He who would be effective in winning people to Christ should employ the Law. Dr. J. Gresham Machen, eminent apologist of an earlier generation, put it this way, "Men would have little difficulty with the Gospel if they had only learned the lesson of the Law." Yes, "the strength of sin is the Law" (1 Cor. 15:56).

A college senior, desiring to become a Christian, protested that he felt no sense of sin and thus no need of the Saviour. A classmate advised, "Go to your room, lock your door, get down on your knees and read the Ten Commandments."

A little later the senior came bounding into his classmate's room exclaiming, "It worked! Before I had finished reading half of the commandments, I saw that I was a sinner and needed a Saviour!"

A friend who observed the senior become an effective minister, delighting in preaching both Law and Gospel, commented, "Much of his power may have been due to his personal experience in discovering the Christ of the cross by reading the Ten Commandments in the spirit of prayer."

The history of preaching bears out the use of the Ten Commandments by the Holy Spirit to produce conviction of sin. Jonathan Edwards was a fiery preacher of law, but on the dark background of its awful penalties he raised the luminous cross of Christ.

John Knox thundered against the breaking of the Decalogue, of which fashionable society and lowly commoner in Scotland were both guilty in his day.

John Wesley advised his fellow preachers, in unfolding their message, to speak first in general of the love of God to man; then, with all possible energy and so as to search conscience to its depths, to preach the law of holiness; and then, and not till then, to uplift the glories of the Gospel of pardon and of life.

One of D. L. Moody's finest series of sermons was "Weighed and Found Wanting," an exposition of the Ten Commandments.

Who hasn't heard Billy Graham on some TV crusade go down the commandments one by one, showing how everyone has broken them all, and then pointing to the blood of Jesus as the only answer? Law precedes the Gospel and leads to Christ. "Christ is the end of the law for righteousness to everyone that believeth" (Rom. 10:4).

For years Paul tried to earn salvation through obedience to the law. One day the woeful inadequacy of his own righteousness led him to trust in the redemption of the only Righteous One. He declared that he wished to "be found in Him [Christ], not having mine own righteousness, which is of the law, but that which is through the faith of Christ, the righteousness which is of God by faith" (Phil. 3:9).

Law is serviceable on the highway to grace. The Law proclaims the bad news that readies the heart for the Good News.

The Ten Commandments as a Regulator of Christian Behavior
Besides summarizing morality, restraining evil, and revealing sin, the Decalogue also gives guidelines for Christian ethical living. "But," objects someone, "doesn't that make this age a legal dispensation instead of the age of liberty? Hasn't the Law been

abrogated? Don't we sing, 'Free from the law, O happy condition'? Doesn't Paul say that we are not under law but under grace?"

We are free from the Law in two respects. First, we are liberated from obligation to keep it as a way to heaven. Because we were utterly incompetent to obey the Law and thus earn heaven, Christ came to earn salvation for us. He perfectly obeyed the Law, then gave His life-blood in payment for our Law-violations. His active and passive obedience together abolished the need for Law-keeping as a condition for salvation. Paul's words, "Ye are not under the law, but under grace" contrast two methods of justification (Rom. 6:14). We cannot be justified by Law-keeping; thus we need forgiveness through grace.

Second, we are free from the Law's punishment. A curse rests on all who fail to keep the whole Law completely. That curse, which should have fallen on violators, Christ received as the Substitute for those who acknowledge Him as Saviour. No longer under the condemning penalty of the Law, we rejoice under the rescue of grace.

But the Law has never been abrogated as a standard of conduct. Since the Christian still lives in perpetual touch with his old nature, he needs a constant reminder of his duty. The Law acts as a molding influence to a Christian character as a call to sanctification. Paul writes, "This is the will of God, even your sanctification," then virtually rephrases the seventh commandment, "that ye should abstain from fornication" (1 Thes. 4:3).

Some say, "No law for us. We obey what is right out of love and by the Holy Spirit." But what is the right they obey out of love and by the Spirit—unless it be the Law of God? There are three major attitudes a Christian may adopt toward the Decalogue.

We earn salvation by obeying the Law—this is legalism and unscriptural.

We deny that the Law is binding on Christian conduct—this is antinomianism and also unscriptural.

We believe that the Law, though not the means of our salvation, is nevertheless a rule of behavior, valid for believers who are empowered by the spirit and motivated by love and gratitude to Christ for their salvation given them apart from the Law.

Two things are required for intelligent Christian living: a clear knowledge of duty and a conscientious practice of it. Though there may be knowledge without obedience, there cannot be consistent obedience without knowledge. This knowledge is gleaned in summary form from the Ten Commandments, whch the Holy Spirit inspired to be repeated and rephrased in many places and ways through the pages of the New Testament.

The Old Testament speaks of three types of law: ceremonial, judicial, and moral. The ceremonial law pertained to sacrifices and offerings and methods of purifications and cleansings. Typical of the coming Messiah, these were fulfilled in the once-for-all sacrifice of Christ, at whose death the curtain to the Holy of Holies was ripped in two from top to bottom as if by a divine hand to show that the ceremonial system was no longer in effect. The abrogation of the ceremonial law is the theme of the Epistle to the Hebrews, who are urged to go on with Christ, the One superior to the old ways.

The judicial law consisted of regulations which God gave the Jews for their civil government. Like the ceremonial law, this system is not binding on us.

The Moral Law—the Ten Commandments—embodies precepts which carry a universal demand. The Decalogue is really a transcript of the Law which God at creation stamped on the moral nature of man (Rom. 2:15). The Moral Law, therefore, was not basically new at the time of Sinai, nor was it exclusively for Israel, but rather for the whole world. This is why all the commandments are repeated many times in the New Testament (except the Sabbath, which is not mentioned because of its ceremonial aspect; this is not to say that the moral aspect is not binding today, namely that part of our time should be devoted especially to God).

An erroneous dichotomy equates the Old Testament with law, and the New Testament with grace. But the Old Testament is full of God's grace in dealing with penitent people, and the New is full of moral law. For example, at the outset of His ministry, Jesus said in the Sermon on the Mount, "I am not come to destroy [the law], but to fulfill" (Matt. 5:17). Then He illustrated His point by expanding two of the commandments, showing that hate is potential murder, a violation of the sixth commandment, and that lustful thinking is potential adultery, a breaking of the seventh commandment. Rather than excusing us from the Law, Christ's application of it to covert thought as well as overt act makes the Decalogue all the more binding.

Paul asks, "Do we then make void the law through faith?" Then he answers, "God forbid; yea, we establish the law" (Rom. 3:31). The meaning could be amplified, "Does not salvation by faith make the law void, lead to its disregard, and open the door to sinful living? To the contrary, the Gospel established the law as a revelation of God's will." Later in the same epistle, Paul wrote, "For I delight in the law of God after the inward man . . . with the mind I myself serve the law of God" (Rom. 7:22, 25).

If the Ten Commandments have become obsolete for believers today, it seems strange that Paul quotes five of them in the practical section of Romans (13:8-9). When he states that "love is the fulfilling of the law" (13:10), he does not mean that love has displaced the commandments, but rather that love provides the motive to obey them. Furthermore, the commandments are avenues down which love expresses itself to neighbors.

A cartoon in *Christianity Today* showed Moses holding the two stone tablets of the Law as he angrily surveys the Israelites worshiping the golden calf Aaron has made. An avant-garde young man says to Moses, "Aaron said perhaps you'd let us reduce them to 'Act responsible in love.' " But the way "responsible love" acts is precisely what the Ten Commandments specify.

It's just as New Testament to preach obedience to the Law as it is to proclaim the death of Christ. When Paul tells children to obey their parents in the Lord, he reinforces the injunction by quoting the fifth commandment, "Honor thy father and mother," and adds, "which is the first commandment with promise" (Eph. 6:1-2). Does not this strongly suggest that the Decalogue continues as a regulator of Christian behavior?

When Paul wrote the Thessalonians he reminded them of previous moral instruction, doubtless given at the time he established the church: "For ye know what commandments we gave you by the Lord Jesus" (1 Thes. 4:2). Dr. Harold J. Ockenga comments, "These commandments were given under the authority of Christ, but they were not Paul's own invention. I am convinced that they were the Ten Commandments for I do not believe that the moral standard has ever been abrogated. It is as permanent and as eternal as the nature of God" (*The Church in God,* Revell, Old Tappan, N.J., 1946).

Vague generalizations about sin are ineffective. We need specific admonitions and prohibitions. The Decalogue is pointed, each commandment beginning with a short sentence like the warning shot of a policeman's revolver. An eminent preacher about to walk to the platform of a church where he was to preach its 100th anniversary sermon, asked the pastor if he should avoid any particular theme. "No," replied the pastor, "you can speak on almost anything here with one exception. My congregation is fond of powerful sermons, but—if you don't mind my saying so—leave the Ten Commandments alone, because they have a most depressing effect on this town!"

Summing up, to preach justification by law is legalistic, voiding the Gospel. To preach the non-validity of the law is antinomian, voiding the law. To preach obedience to the law for the Christian who has been justified apart from the law, is evangelical, voiding neither grace nor law.

Though the believer is not under the law's condemning power, he is under its commanding power. The law does not give, but it does guide, life.

The Ten Commandments as a Road Map to Happiness

To many, the Ten Commandments seem joy-killers. But the opposite is true—rather than dulling life, they give it delight. God gave the Decalogue because He loves us, not because He wants to hamper our happiness. To disobey the commandments leads to loss of joy and sometimes to the psychiatrist's office. Obedience yields the abundant life.

Each commandment could be phrased as a beatitude. For example, "Blessed is the man who does not lie. Blessed are those who do not steal." God, who made us, knows best how we should operate to know maximum happiness. Just as an appliance is often accompanied by a book of directions which tells how it will run best, so man's Creator has given a direction-book, the Bible, which tells man how to live so as to achieve maximum satisfaction. This direction-book stresses the Ten Commandments, and blessed is the person who follows them. Indeed, in the midst of giving the commandments, God promised to show mercy to those who "keep My commandments" (Ex. 20:6).

Dr. Cyrus Gordon, Hebrew scholar and professor of Near Eastern Studies at Brandeis University, says:

> The Ten Commandments are a landmark in human history, because they sum up in a few verses so much of what society and the individual need for a good, orderly, and productive life. If we were to follow these sacred precepts, we would become as free as possible from the turmoil that results from transgression, and from the dissatisfaction that stems from coveting. We would have a more stable society in which parents and children would be better united in respect and love. We would be more atune to the divine order of things through following the commandments of God.

Modern man, skeptical of the origin, authority, and workability of the Decalogue, wants to work out his own code of behavior. But Dr. Gordon states:

> In the process of rediscovering time-honored, tested, and self-evident truth, we can fritter away much of our lifetime. Relativism in morality and ethics tends to deflect a man from his work and sometimes renders him in need of psychic therapy as well. The man who accepts the Ten Commandments as absolute has a better chance of being released for efficient work during six days, and refreshed on the Sabbath, every week ("The Ten Commandments," *Christianity Today*, April 10, 1964).

Some argue that the Ten Commandments are old-fashioned. So is the law of gravity, but anyone who jumps from a height will get hurt. As will anyone defying the Decalogue. A prisoner, breaking up rocks in a jailyard, remarked to a visiting minister, "The Ten Commandments are like hard rock. But you don't break them; rather you break yourself against them!"

The commandments may seem narrow, but so does every runway on airports all around the world. Yet no passenger wants his pilot to miss the narrow runway and land a few yards off the mark in some field or waterway or row of houses. The narrow ribbon of pavement is really the broad way that leads to a safe, comfortable landing. So the seemingly rigid Decalogue guides to happy, fulfilled living.

Violations bring their penalties. A *Reader's Digest* article says:
On basic issues of right and wrong, the essential values are what they have always been. To kill, to steal, to lie, or to covet another person's possessions still leads to varying degrees of misery for the victim and the perpetrator. The 20th century has not found a way to repeal the Ten Commandments. "Thou shalt not commit adultery" may sound old-fashioned, but restated in contemporary terms—"Do not smash up another person's family life"—it still carries a worthwhile message (William V. Shannon, "What Code of Values Can We Teach Our Children Now?" *Reader's Digest,* May 1972).

A competent and experienced English psychiatrist has written a book on the importance of the Ten Commandments in the field of mental health. In *Psychiatry, The Ten Commandments, and You* (Dodd, Meade, & Co., N.Y.), Dr. Sydney Sharman, not a professing Christian, asserts that the Decalogue is just as relevant to man today as when first set down on tablets of stone. He supports the thesis that a life-style based on the Ten Commandments reduces immeasurably the vulnerability of an individual to neurotic ill health. Not only does the Decalogue offer a basis of prevention, but also a cure for many of modern man's neuroses. Using several case histories, and devoting a separate chapter to each of the commandments, the psychiatrist illustrates how he has been able to help some of his patients, not by probing into the depth of the subconscious so much as by confronting the conscious mind with the principles and standards of the Ten Commandments.

Such pronouncements from psychiatrists should not surprise us as Christians. God promised wholeness to all those who would keep His law at the time He gave it!

A Methodist superintendent commented:
The Ten Commandments are not arbitrary commands forced upon us; they are a revelation of truth to be followed. This is the way life is structured. If history is faltering today, it is not because the Ten Commandments have failed, but because civilization is disregarding its life principles. Someone has suggested that "sin is trying to get more out of life than there is in it!"

Fulfillment issues from following life principles; shortcuts lead only to mirage and disappointment. "You can do what is wrong; but you can't make it work" (Robert G. Tuttle, "Ten Essential Life Principles," *Christianity Today*).

"Oh that there were such an heart in them, that they would fear Me, and keep all My commandments always, *that it might be well with them,* and with their children forever!" (Deut. 5:29)

2

God Will Not Play
Second Fiddle

Commandment One: "Thou shalt have no other
gods before Me" (Ex. 20:3).

A man purchased a statue of Christ at an auction, and placed it on the desk in his den. A few days later his wife moved the statue to a table in the living room. Their five-year-old daughter, noticing the change of location, blurted out, "Where are you going to put God?"

The first commandment leaves no doubt as to the position God wants in our lives. He demands our first allegiance. He will not play second fiddle. He commands, "Thou shalt have no other gods before Me."

The commandments begin where any Christian system must start, where the Bible begins, with God. Since God is Creator, Sustainer, and Preserver, how natural to make Him the starting point. On Him we are dependent; to Him we are responsible. Where God is not properly honored, degradation follows. The first chapter of Romans traces the appalling shipwreck that results when God is thrown overboard.

A striking difference between the Ten Commandments and other codes of law, like those of Hammurabi and the Hittites, which antedate the Mosaic code by centuries, is the Decalogue's demand for the recognition of God. Though other codes reach out horizontally man to man with civil laws involving such matters as banking, sale of property, slavery, wages, and taxation, they neglect the all-important, primary, vertical relationship of man to God. That the Decalogue stresses first and foremost love to God both shows its superiority over other codes and strengthens our belief in its divine origin.

Not only does the first command presuppose a belief in God, which rules out atheism, but it is preceded by an emphatic theistic declaration, "And God spake all these words, saying, 'I am the Lord thy God which have brought thee out of the land of Egypt, out of the house of bondage'" (Ex. 20:1-2).

With one deft stroke the first law knocks out several enemies of theism: not only atheism, but polytheism, ignorance, and idolatry.

It Rules out Polytheism

Polytheism, far more than atheism, has been man's problem throughout history. Rather than be without deity, man has believed in a host of gods: a god of the mountain, a god of the river, a god of the forest, of spring planting, of harvest, of childbirth, of the sun, the moon, fire, fishermen, wind—an endless line of deities. Man must have an object of worship and does—too many of them. At one time or other man has worshiped dogs, serpents, vermin, and cows, to name a few.

Israel's survival necessitated a death-blow to polytheism. Egypt, among the most polytheistic nations history has known, boasted over 2,000 different gods and goddesses. To prove His superiority over these gods, God directed some if not all of the 10 plagues (Ex. 7—12) against particular deities.

For example, the Nile River was an object of worship. Believed to be of heavenly origin, the Nile was worshiped in prayer and song, the people lauding it as the indispensable lord and helper of the poor and needy. When Moses smote the Nile to turn it into blood in the first plague, the Nile was shown to be inferior to God.

The frog, also an Egyptian deity, was humiliated in the second plague by its spread in beds, walks, and food troughs. Similarly, the fifth plague disgraced another important goddess, the cow, by inflicting Egypt's cattle with murrain, a plague similar to anthrax or Texas fever.

A higher stage of polytheism, known as henotheism, centers in the worship of only one god by a nation which at the same time accepts the gods of other nations as real. A god was supreme within its own boundaries, but other gods were acknowledged as valid in other territories. Intermarriage between royalty of nations with differing gods always added another god to each nation's worship. Solomon's many wives introduced many new gods into Solomon's kingdom, thus polluting the worship of God. Jezebel also brought her strange gods to complicate Israel's religious scene.

The first commandment forbids polytheism in any and every form. It took the Babylonian captivity nine centuries later to cure Israel of her many departures from belief in the one and only true God.

It Rules out Ignorance of God

A pamphlet published by the United Nations on its "Meditation Room" at its New York City headquarters says of the stone in the middle of the room, "We may see it as an altar, empty not because there is no god, but because it is dedicated to the God whom man worships under many names and in many forms." This subtle polytheism points up the imperfection of man's concepts of God apart from divine help.

If we could keep the first commandment, which orders us to esteem God above all other gods, we must learn all we can about Him. To honor God requires an intelligent appraisal of the Almighty through diligent study of His nature, attributes, and works. Knowledge of God, not ignorance, provides the basis for pledging supreme allegiance to Him.

Where can we derive this knowledge? From the revelation God has given of Himself in His Word. Based on His self-revelation in the Bible, the Westminster Shorter Catechism gives what has been called the best definition of God ever penned by man: "God is a Spirit, infinite, eternal, and unchangeable in His being, wisdom, power, holiness, justice, goodness, and truth."

At age 21 Charles H. Spurgeon made this keen observation as he began a series of studies on the nature and character of God, "It has been said that the 'proper study of mankind is man.' I will not oppose the idea, but I believe it is equally true that the proper study of God's elect is God. The highest science, the loftiest speculation, the mightiest philosophy, which can ever engage the attention of a child of God, is the name, the nature, the person, the work, the doings, and the existence of the great God whom he calls his Father."

An erroneous view of God can lead to a wrong course of behavior. In the ancient world the god Baal was believed to be the source of growth, the most mysterious form of which was the power to beget a child. Since the power of sex was attributed to Baal, the sex act became a sacred deed. Baal's temples were thronged with priestesses who were sacred prostitutes. Sexual involvement with one of the "holy women" was union with the life-force of the god Baal. Immorality thus became worship, a strong attraction for fallen human nature. No wonder the Decalogue begins by emphasizing the only true God, with the implication we should learn all we can about Him.

Though we can never learn all there is to know about God, for His thoughts are not our thoughts and He lives in light to which no can can approach, we may know enough to acclaim Him superior and supreme. Increased understanding of His nature, power, majesty, and glory will give ample reason for bowing in humility and esteeming Him above all.

It Rules out Idolatry

Not only should we learn about the one and only true God, but we should never let anyone or anything usurp His place of absolute priority in our lives. The possibility of idolatry always looms as a danger, for man must worship something. Like the flow of a river which cannot be stopped but which can be diverted, the yearning of man's soul for an object of worship can easily turn from the true God to another god.

Idolatry may be external or internal. Multitudes in the western world who would never think of crassly bowing to gods of wood and stone (external idolatry), nevertheless give their allegiance to gods, just as lifeless and empty, which they set up in their hearts (internal idolatry). An idol is anything we put before God.

A few years ago *Christianity Today* asked a panel of Christian scholars, "What are the most prevalent false gods of our time?"

Those mentioned included the anti-Christian welfare state, scientism, Communism, political democracy, nationalism, conservatism (inordinate regard for what one already has), social adjustment, behaviorism, secularism, humanism, naturalism, and the cult of progress.

Some more personal idols were listed by Dr. Andrew W. Blackwood, professor emeritus of Princeton Theological Seminary, who said, "In America today false gods abound. They call for perversion of things ideally good: self, money, pleasure, sex, romance (as in marriage), amusements (commercial), sports (professional), education (secular)." He added, "We need a return to the first commandment, in the light of the Cross."

Let's look at some twentieth-century idols, often enthroned in human hearts in place of God.

Possessions Some idols are chrome-plated. Others involve bucket seats or high-powered engines, or large estates, or gilt-edged securities, or latest fashions. Some display luxuriously panelled walls, a 29″ color screen, famous brand labels. They may be our homes, stamp collections, antiques, or gardens. "The principal false god of our time," according to Dr. W. Stanford Reid, McGill University professor, "is our standard of living. We are so concerned with material possessions that we forget they are the gift of God and that there are other things more important. We may yet have to lose our standard of living or surrender a large part of it before we become aware that there are much more important values. After all, man's chief end in life is to glorify God and to enjoy Him forever, not to have a house with a swimming pool" (*Christianity Today*).

Plenty The almighty dollar easily displaces the Almighty in many hearts. Love of money, or covetousness, is plainly called idolatry by Scripture (Col. 3:5). As wealth increases, we want more. When we enjoy the good life, it's hard to distinguish between needs and greeds.

To store his abundant crops, the rich fool built bigger barns (Luke 12:16-21). To capitalize on its well-watered fields, Lot pitched his tent toward Sodom (Gen. 13:10-12). Some men let business eat up all their energies, time, and capital, relegating everything else, including God, to the background. Even when they attend church, instead of following the sermon they are busy figuring new methods of promoting business. Such a man has more business than he has business to have. Just as a little coin can blot out the sun, if held close to the eye, so the relentless pursuit of security can make us lose sight of God.

As one aid to keep money from climbing the throne of our lives God gave the principle of the tithe. The practice of contributing the first tenth of our income to the Lord's work reminds us to be more giving than grabbing, more sacrifical than selfish. Tithing helps cut the nerve of money-worship.

Pride   A 12-year-old girl, a hunchback, on her first day of school after her family moved to a new section of the city saw a youngster point at her and heard, "Look at the new girl with the crooked back!" When it rained the next morning, the little girl carried a huge black umbrella, effectively hiding her back.

After that the umbrella was always with her, till one day a wise counselor said, "I've heard something that surprises me very much. I've been told that you are the most conceited little girl in our city." When the girl protested, the counselor gently replied, "My dear, whenever you walk out of your house you think everyone is looking at you. Isn't that why you always carry that umbrella?"

The little girl hung her head, then nodded, and promised to leave the umbrella home next day. The following morning, as she walked down the street, for the first time in months without that awkward encumbrance, she realized that no one was looking at her. From that moment on she was freed from her self-consciousness for all time. Too often we are concerned, not by what people think of us, but by what our pride leads us to think they think of us.

Love of self (*I*-doll) may lead to arrogance, boastfulness, vanity, and to excessive interest in one's health, performance, reputation, or appearance. An inferiority complex is related to the first commandment. How often we set up an image of ourself as we would like to be, then feel inferior to others in some way, but each of us is also superior in some way. Thus we need to evaluate both our good and bad points. Humility gives serenity.

Persons   An idol may be a *she*-doll or a *he*-doll. On the tombstone of a little girl, an only child, were chiseled these words: "Her parents put all their wealth in one vessel, and the shipwreck was total." It's possible for parents to so idolize a child that they try to block him from going to the mission field.

How Abraham must have loved Isaac, son of his old age, but he proved he valued God more by his willingness to sacrifice the apple of his eye (Gen. 22:1-14). Hannah, who became a mother after barrenness, did not put little Samuel above the Lord. Rather, at great sacrifice she brought him when still a little child, and her only child then, to the tabernacle to give him back to the Lord. Said Jesus, "He that loveth son or daughter more than Me is not worthy of Me" (Matt. 10:37).

Jesus also said, "He that loveth father or mother more than Me is not worthy of Me." A would-be disciple, invited by Jesus to follow Him, replied, "Lord, suffer me first to go and bury my father." To this apparently noble request Jesus gave a seemingly cruel answer: "Let the dead bury their dead: but go thou and preach the kingdom of God" (Luke 9:59-60). Likely his father had not died, may not even have been sick, and was being used as an excuse for delay. The Lord permits no rivals to take prime slot over Him.

A young man preparing for the mission field fell in love with a Christian girl, who would not consent to becoming a missionary. He surrendered his purpose, married the girl, and became well-to-do. But in his final months, he was heard to say, "The day I gave my consent to remain at home, peace went out of my heart never to return." He had put his girlfriend above God. On the other hand, many young people through the years, faced with an eviction order from their parents unless they surrendered their Christion confession, have chosen Christ over parents and home.

Though no husband can love his wife too much in the proper way, it is possible for a man to do things to please his wife that he knows do not please God. Not Charles H. Spurgeon. Shortly before his marriage, he and his fiancee arrived at a hall where Spurgeon was to preach. They were separated in the jostling crowd of thousands, as he pushed his way to the platform. Arriving at her house after the service, he found her pouting. "I'm sorry," he said, "but perhaps what happened was providential. I did not intend to be impolite, but whenever I see a crowd like that waiting for me to preach, I am overwhelmed with the sense of responsibility. I forgot about you. Now, it will have to be the rule of our marriage that the command of my Master comes first. You shall have the second place. Are you willing, as my wife, to take the second place while I give the first place to Christ?"

A wise woman who genuinely loved her Lord, she answered, "Yes, I'll take the second place."

The Corinthian Christians were divided over their leaders. Some said, "I am of Paul," others "I am of Apollos," and still others "I am of Peter." They were virtually idolizing human beings who were merely servants of God, workers who had received all of their abilities from the Almighty. This is not so much different from some church members today. They enthusiastically support special services featuring big-name singers or preachers with exciting life stories or glamorous talents but fail to attend the regular services of their church. A wise pastor warned his flock, "Never worship any man, for all idols have clay feet."

A nominal Christian wife had a wide circle of friends, some of whom invariably arrived to visit her late Sunday afternoon. Her husband said to his wife, "My dear, I'm not going to dictate what you ought to do, but I want you to understand clearly that I will not permit these social visits to interfere with my duty to God." Sunday after Sunday, just before church time he would say to the visitors, "You'll have to excuse me. It's my practice to attend the house of God every Sunday night. It's a rule I never break, if I can help it. It's time now to go, and if you'll permit, I'll just slip away." Graciously he let them know that God was first.

Willingness to love God more than any other person, whether parent, child, brother, sister, relative or friend, is required by the first commandment.

Pleasure   Everyone needs some diversion from the monotonies of life. But legitimate amusements and innocent pleasures have a way of captivating the heart. The entertainment pages of any city newspaper reveal how deeply the god of pleasure has invaded all areas of society. Devotees by the thousands crowd into arenas, stadiums, movies, and nightclubs. And often they crowd out God.

Some people live solely for a good time, pursuing an endless round of fun. Self-gratification is their deity. The god of pleasure thrives when material prosperity rises and moral standards decay. Sensuality and self-indulgence run rampant in our day. Sex is the chief pursuit of so many that someone said the time in America is sex o'clock!

Paul warned that people will be "lovers of pleasures more than lovers of God" (2 Tim. 3:4). We need more committed people like Moses who chose "rather to suffer affliction with the people of God, than to enjoy the pleasures of sin for a season" (Heb. 11:25).

Projects   Some folks get all wrapped up in worthy causes which become their total life: a political party, Little League, the arts, the fire department, the PTA, "world peace," or "freedom from want." One's all-consuming passion might be a profession or hobby, a vocation or avocation. Strangely, one's idol could even be a religious project: "the biggest Sunday School in the area," or "the best attended morning service in town," or "the most active youth group in the city," or "the best missionary giving church in the denomination."

Peter, Andrew, James, and John did not let their fishing partnership interfere with duty to God. When Christ called them, they left their trade—nets, fish, fathers, and all. Matthew the tax collector heard Jesus say "Follow Me," and left his lucrative business in busy Capernaum, plus his ledgers, debits, and credits. These disciples could say,

> I heard His call, "Come follow,"
> That was all.
> My gold grew dim,
> My soul went after Him,
> I rose and followed.
> That was all.
> Who would not follow
> If they heard Him call?

Prominence   Some worship status. Like the Pharisees of Jesus' day who sought out the chief seats at banquets, they want to sit at the head table. Others want to be in *Who's Who* or the social register, or have their names in the newspaper often, or have buildings, rooms, or avenues named after them. Some dream of seeing their names in bright lights, or given top billing in a list of credits. Still others crave a presidency or chairmanship, so they can revel in the prestige, position, and power. This is their life, their all.

A woman with a well-known ancestry asked a new neighbor in town if her forefathers had come over on the *Mayflower*. Tipped off in advance to this woman's worship of pedigree, the neighbor replied, "No, but they were there to meet the boat!"

Dr. Merrill C. Tenney, Dean Emeritus of the Wheaton College Graduate School, says, "Prestige, possessions, power, and pleasures are the false gods of modern man. They represent a tragic devotion to material gain rather than to spiritual good, to transient gratification rather than to eternal values. They are as futile and unsatisfying to the spirit as an idol of wood or of stone" (*Christianity Today*). All these gods will end up on the ash heap of a burned-out and empty life.

Easy to Lapse into Idolatry

How easy it is to crowd God off the throne as some secondary interest eases into His place! A parable tells of an idol-burning ceremony in the backyard of a church. Each person had torn from his heart his dearest possession, ambition, or achievement and had placed it on a heap with the other idols: long hair, new Ph.D., antique, not-yet-purchased mink coat. But no one could find a match. However, all agreed that failure to burn them didn't mean they weren't giving them up. Slowly the group drifted homeward, with one or two backward glances. One woman didn't sleep well that night and at last convinced herself that what she had given up was no idol. Early the next morning she sneaked back to the great pile of idols, hoping not to be seen. When she got there, she found her idol, lonely and forlorn, the only one still left.

Robert E. Speer was a missionary statesman for nearly half a century. Previously he had been an outstanding athlete at Princeton, where he played four years on the university football team, a sport he dearly loved. A few years after his graduation, a friend who knew of his interest in sports invited him to a football game. Speer refused, giving this reason. He had gone to one game after entering foreign missionary service and had become so absorbed in the game and stirred so emotionally by it that for many days afterward he could not concentrate on his work. Thereupon he decided not to attend any more games in that sport in which he had excelled and which he loved so deeply.

The first commandment should lead us to pray with the hymn-writer,

> *The dearest idol I have known,*
> *Whate'er that idol be,*
> *Help me to tear it from its throne*
> *And worship only Thee.*

How up-to-date is John's concluding advice in the final verse of his first epistle, "Little children, keep yourselves from idols" (1 John 5:21).

3

With All Thy Strength

Commandment Two: "Thou shalt not make unto thee any graven image" (Ex. 20:4).

A wealthy man in the Orient rented his large house to tenants, but reserved one room for his gods. Placing them all in that one room, he locked the door. Much later he came back and opened the door to get his gods, but all he saw was dust. White ants had eaten them.

The worship of gods fashioned by man, whether of wood or stone, metal or bone, is not only futile but forbidden by the second commandment: "Thou shalt not make unto thee any graven image, or any likeness of anything that is in heaven above, or that is in the earth beneath, or that is in the water under the earth. Thou shalt not bow down thyself to them, nor serve them" (Ex. 20:4-5).

Idolatry may be either internal or external. To cherish on the shelf of our heart anything that displaces our affection for God constitutes internal idolatry and is prohibited by the first commandment. The erection and veneration of visible objects of worship comprises external idolatry, which receives its death-blow in the second commandment.

Image-worship Forbidden

Is it wrong to make images, statues, or replicas of anything that moves in the air, in the sea, or on the earth? Some interpret this command so strictly that they refuse to adorn their homes. They reject not only statuary, but pictures, photographs, stuffed animals, and dolls.

A traveler in the Holy Land told how a bust of General Allenby, which stood in the middle of a group of parched little trees in Beersheba, was hated by the Bedouins. Though they admired brave warriors, they rejected all sculptured images, based on literal acceptance of the second commandment. If crops withered or rains failed or pestilence struck, these Bedouins looked the other way when passing the bust of Lord Allenby.

If all visible representations are forbidden, then the Lord's instructions for the building of the tabernacle contradict His own injunction. The curtain hanging before the Holy of Holies was adorned with cherubic figures. Images of cherubim overshadowed the Ark of the Covenant. The golden candlestick took the form of a tree. The hem of the high priest's garment was decorated with likenesses of pomegranates alternating with bells.

Later, Solomon's temple, adorned with carved figures of cherubim, palm trees, and open flowers, enjoyed the presence of God, an inexplicable paradox if God were displeased with the making of visible representations.

The art gift comes from God. Made in the image of God, man has an aesthetic nature which impels him to create and enjoy the beautiful. God made the universe; man makes a sort of cosmos in the monuments of architecture. God made the landscape, which man tries to reproduce in painting. God made the forms of nature; man attempts to follow suit through sculpture.

To make an image is no sin; the iniquity arises from worshiping it. We admire "the ingenuity in making" but decry "the stupidity in worshiping." This command could be paraphrased, "Thou shalt not make anything with the intent to worship it. Neither shalt thou worship anything which others have made."

According to an extra-biblical story, Abraham's father was an idol-maker back in Ur of the Chaldees. One day, after a confrontation by God, Abraham destroyed every image in his father's shop except a lovely little deity seated on a pedestal. In the hands of this cute god, Abraham placed the hammer with which he had destroyed the others. When his angry father demanded to know who had destroyed the gods, Abraham pointed to the little god. "Ask him. He has a hammer." When the father replied that the god could not speak, Abraham drove home his point. "That's exactly what I'm trying to show you. A living God is not one fashioned into an image, but One who can speak, and whom we must heed."

How absurd to worship an inanimate thing whose eyes see not, whose ears hear not, whose mouth speaks not. Yet millions the world over are bewitched by idols. Man seems to require an external aid to worship, so he manufactures a visible god. Even as Moses was descending Sinai with the Decalogue which forbade the worship of graven images, the Israelites were dancing around a golden calf (Ex. 32).

To kneel, pray, or burn incense before any statue, whether saint or angel or image of Christ, is hard to reconcile with the command, "Thou shalt not bow down thyself to them." In European cathedrals toes have been worn smooth on many images through constant kissing by devotees.

Some theologians excuse bowing to images, claiming that genuflection is not to the image, which is only a representation, but to the person whom the image represents. But this theological distinction often eludes the genuflecter. First-century heathen defended their deference to images on similar grounds, but the early Christians called the practice idolatrous.

An idol has been called a paradoxical thing. How ludicrous on the one hand that man should view as a god something which he himself has chopped down and shaped, something which has to be carried, if fallen over cannot lift itself, can be smudged by temple smoke, must be locked up at night lest it be stolen. Yet on the other hand, may worship of the invisible God be easier if we carve a little image to remind us of Him? No, despite noble intent, before long instead of focusing our attention on God whom it supposedly represents, the image begins more and more to take the place of God.

How easy for a thing to become an object of worship. For example, the bronze serpent set up by Moses to heal those bitten by fiery serpents was later broken in pieces by King Hezekiah because the people had been burning incense to it (2 Kings 18:4). What was meant to be a reminder of God became a god.

Those who use a crucifix to recall the sufferings of Christ should beware lest it become an object of superstitious adoration, thus confusing symbol with reality.

Even the worship of the true God with the aid of images is forbidden. Why is it wrong to worship God through images? Because God is infinite and cannot be circumscribed by lines. God is invisible and cannot be represented adequately. A likeness of a creature is not a likeness of its Creator. Any such representation corrupts the glory of God. The adulterated figure makes Him out to be other than He is. Says Dr. Harold Lindsell, editor of *Christianity Today,*

> The infinite, invisible God cannot be limited to plastic forms nor be truly represented in any man-made fashion. Graven images profess to give men some real idea of what God is like. This cannot be done; for if the whole world were filled with figures of God they would all give the wrong impression, and there would not be enough of them to begin to fill the need. God is a spirit, and any endeavor by man to anthropomorphize Him does violence to His being and person. Such efforts end up humanizing God and bringing Him down to the level of men. No artificial image, however conceived, has ever succeeded in lifting God above what He is or even come close to conveying His reality (*The World, the Flesh, and the Devil,* Canon Press, Washington, D.C.).

None of us likes to have in circulation poor pictures of ourselves. Rather we give our friends what we consider good likenesses. Similarly, God does not like a poor or false replica of Himself, which every image of deity is. Images are really unlikenesses of God, not likenesses.

Another consideration against the use of images in worship is that they violate the relationship between God and His people. According to Old Testament prophets, the worship of idols constituted infidelity, which God termed spiritual adultery, provoking Him to vengeance (Deut. 32:21; 1 Kings 14:22-23; Ezek. 8:3). The second commandment carries this warning, "I the Lord thy God am a jealous God, visiting the iniquity of the fathers upon the children unto the third and fourth generation of them that hate Me" (Ex. 20:5).

Israel had to learn the hard way. Though rebuked by prophets time and again, princes and people sought heathen deities. At one time the situation was so bad that only 7,000 citizens had not bowed the knee to Baal (1 Kings 19:18). Repeated minor punishments, not long heeded, finally culminated in the captivities, which effected a permanent cure. External idolatry was never a sin of later Judaism.

Apostolic preaching condemned idolatry. Paul's mission at Ephesus gradually destroyed the silversmiths' lucrative business of making Diana replicas (Acts 19:23-27). The exclusion of images continued for three centuries till Emperor Constantine proclaimed Christianity the state religion in A.D. 325. This opened the door to an influx of unconverted heathen who introduced pagan customs into the church, among them the adoration of idols. Though some early councils condemned the use of images in church worship, the Nicene Council of A.D. 787 not only permitted image veneration, but pronounced a curse on all opposing the practice. That policy then flourished till the Reformation.

The Reformers stood as a bulwark against idol-worship. Though the leaders disapproved of violent, forcible removal of images from churches, groups of extremists and fanatics frequently took the matter into their own hands, breaking into churches and destroying objects of adoration.

Some Reformers permitted the use of images for instruction. However, all united on their exclusion for purposes of worship. G. Campbell Morgan mentions that in his day in Westminster Abbey a great many statues were removed from their niches by the authorities because worshippers burnt lamps and knelt before them, not simply because they were statues (*The Ten Commandments,* Revell, Old Tappan, N.J.).

In the Lutheran and Catholic listings of the commandments the first two are merged into one, and counted as the first commandment. In order to make 10, the total stated by the Bible (Ex. 34:28), Lutheran and Catholic enumeration divides the tenth into two: "Thou shalt not covet thy neighbor's wife" and "Thou shalt not covet thy neighbor's house." This separation of the "covet" command not only seems a strained arrangement, but also often results in the de-emphasis of the second commandment. In fact, some abbreviated catechisms omit this prohibition entirely, going from "no other gods" to "not taking God's name in vain" without mention of "not bowing down to graven images."

The central truth of Christianity, the incarnation of Jesus Christ, is related to the second commandment. God has revealed Himself, not in shapes of wood or stone, but in human form—in the unique person of Jesus Christ, who possessed two natures—the divine and the human. This God-man demonstrated by deed and word what God was like. That's why He could say, "He that hath seen Me hath seen the Father" (John 14:9).

Though we are to "flee from idolatry" (1 Cor. 10:14), we are to follow Christ who is "the image of the invisible God" (Col. 1:15).

Irregularities in Worship Prohibited

We ought not to worship God in ways other than those which He has enjoined us. By implication, this command forbids any irregularity in our worship of the true God.

When Nadab and Abihu, sons of Aaron, offered strange fire before the Lord, "which He commanded not," fire from the Lord devoured them (Lev. 10:1-2).

Some attend church with ulterior motives—for example, to keep face in the community or to meet prospects for business. One merchant whose denomination differed from his wife's insisted they keep attending their separate churches so as to embrace a wider circle of potential customers. To worship so men will note our presence is really to worship man and his opinions, not God. It's like the hypocrites who blew trumpets to attract attention to their piety (Matt. 6:1-4).

Some go to church to see people rather than to commune with God. A Washington pastor whose church was attended now and again by the president of the United States received a phone call asking, "Can you tell me if the president is expected to attend church next Sunday?"

"That," the pastor patiently replied, "I cannot promise, but we do expect God to be present, and we fancy that will be sufficient incentive for a reasonably large attendance."

Whenever we exalt liturgies, creeds, forms of ecclesiastical government, or church buildings, idolatry threatens. To go through forms of worship perfunctorily, to say prayers we don't feel, to sing hymns we don't mean, to render solos simply because we're paid, to give money because we're being watched or only because it's deductible for income tax purposes, all these fall below genuine worship of the true God.

It's like the husband and wife who compared notes on the morning service as they sat at Sunday dinner. The wife asked, "Did you notice the mink coat on the lady in front of us today?"

"No," confessed the husband, "I was dozing."

Retorted the wife, "A lot of good the sermon did you!"

The second commandment requires worship in spirit and in truth (John 4:24).

The Puritans classified as an idolator anyone who worshiped the devil, or who worshiped objects of nature such as the sun, moon, or stars, or who prayed to saint or angel.

The Puritans also included superstition as a violation of this command. All who trust more in anything other than God are idolators, whether it be rabbit's foot, tea leaves, crystal ball, the crossing of fingers, or refusing to walk a path crossed by a black cat.

To give credence to astrology and the occult instead of to the Word of God would be ruled out by the implications of the second commandment.

Inertness with Regard to Worship Forbidden

Not only does the second commandment forbid image-worship and irregularities in worship, but it also condemns idleness, inactivity, and indolence in connection with worship.

Following the rule of interpretation that negative commands may be stated positively, this one would read, "Thou shalt bow down to the one true God." The same sort of physical deference, or outward obeisance which heathen give to false gods, should be given by Christians to the living God. The same sort of energies expended in the worship of false deities should be devoted to the service of the true God.

A missionary comments that Muslims faithfully observe their stated times of prayer, even when quite ill. Though prayer for them involves much physical exercise, they alternately stand erect, bend forward, sit on their heels, and touch the ground with their forehead, despite their ailments. Should not those who know God through Jesus Christ be delighted to honor Him with their bodies, their physical powers, their strength?

The first commandment sums up our highest duty to God—to have no other gods before Him—to love Him supremely. The next three, second, third, and fourth, indicate directions in which this supreme love should express itself.

First	*LOVE GOD SUPREMELY*	—no other gods
Second	—with your strength	—bowing to the true God
Third	—with your speech	—not using God's name vainly
Fourth	—with your sabbaths	—remembering the Sabbath Day

God has made the whole man, body as well as spirit, for Himself. Believers' bodies are the temples of the Holy Spirit. Therefore we are to glorify God in our bodies (1 Cor. 6:19-20).

When the Sunday morning bells toll the invitation to church, perhaps the temptation to enjoy a couple more hours of sleep wins out. One may think, *I'll tune in a church broadcast.* Thus the spirit travels to divine worship while the body remains in bed, attending "the church of the pillow and sheets." The spirit is willing, but the flesh is weak. The second commandment requires the attendance of body as well as of spirit.

A town skinflint tried to squirm out of buying tickets for an ambulance-benefit organ recital. "I'll be with you in spirit," he offered. The fund raiser retorted as he waved several tickets in his hand, "Fine, how far back in the auditorium does your spirit wish to sit?"

Spirits without bodies cannot fill pews, sing hymns, pass collection plates, dig in purses or pockets for offerings, lend ears to sermons, bow heads in prayer, lift bread or cup to mouths in the Lord's Supper.

Bodies comfortably parked by a fireplace with Sunday newspaper or football game on TV cannot be ministering at the nursing home or bringing cheer to shut-ins. Bodies lolling around some cook-out or loafing by a swimming-pool cannot at the same time support the evening service. Likewise, those who claim to worship God on a golf course or to the smell of gasoline on the open highway forget that the complete man doesn't participate in such worship. Even if the spirit could quietly and sincerely commune with God amid such distractions, the energies of the body are being spent in obeisance to the gods of sport and fun. True worship demands transporting our bodies to be with other bodies of God's people in corporate worship (Heb. 10:25).

The Lord's work demands strength. It took energy for Dorcas to sew garments for needy widows (Acts 9:39). It took stamina for Onesiphorus to seek Paul out diligently when he was a prisoner in Rome, probably in the dreaded Mamertine jail, and to bring refreshment to the incarcerated apostle (2 Tim. 1:16-17).

It will mean using our vitality to work in our church visitation program, teach a Sunday School class of active children, act as sponsor of a youth group, give a cup of cold water in Jesus' name, give food to the hungry, show hospitality to a stranger, or visit the sick or prisoner.

So many of our energies these days are devoted to the false gods of status: impressive homes, furniture, hobbies, cars, careers, money. What a shot in the arm the church would receive if people would transfer the same intensity to the extension of God's kingdom. Lukewarmness, limpness, and lethargy are rebuked by the second commandment. Rather, we are to present our bodies as living sacrifices (Rom. 12:1-2).

A little boy affirmed that he loved his mother with all his strength. Asked to explain what he meant by "all his strength," he answered, "We live on the fourth floor of our building and there's no elevator. We don't have central heating. We have a coal stove and the coal is kept down in the basement. Mother is very busy most of the time, and besides, she isn't very strong; so I see to it that the coal scuttle is never empty. I haul the coal up four flights of stairs, all by myself, and it's a pretty big load. It takes all my strength to get it up there. Now isn't that loving my mother with all my strength?"

Jesus said, "Thou shalt love the Lord thy God with all thy heart, and with all thy soul, and with *all thy strength,* and with all thy mind" (Luke 10:27).

4

"Hallowed Be Thy Name"

Commandment Three: "Thou shalt not take the name of the Lord . . . in vain" (Ex. 20:7).

During World War II American soldiers on a Pacific Island were startled to read this announcement posted at the entrance to their mess hall:

"American soldiers are requested please to be a little more careful in their choice of language, especially when nationals are assisting them in unloading ships and trucks and in erecting abodes.

"American missionaries spent many years among us and taught us the use of clean speech. Every day, however, American soldiers use bad words, and the good work your missionaries did in our midst is being undermined by your careless profanity."

The notice was signed by a Polynesian chief.

About 3,500 years ago the Lord Himself published a notice to all mankind. It reads, "Thou shalt not take the name of the Lord thy God in vain" (Ex. 20:7).

In biblical usage, a name was an expression of character standing for the person. To trust in the name of God was to trust in God. *Vain* means empty, idle, insincere, phony, frivolous, lacking in reality or truth. It is used of a false report. To take God's name in vain would be to treat God lightly, irreverently, or insincerely. The commandment warns us that in all of our words we should be aware of the reality of God.

The first four commandments portray our duty to God. The

first sums it up as love; then the next three give ways of expressing that supreme love.

First	LOVE GOD SUPREMELY	—no other gods
Second	—by prostration of body	—not bowing to the false
Third	—by profession of mouth	—not taking His name vainly
Fourth	—by proffering of time	—remembering sabbaths

Ways We May Take God's Name in Vain
Men violate this commandment in many different ways.

By lying under oath   Oaths may be made formally in court,
or informally out of court. In either case God's Word says, "Ye
shall not swear by My name falsely" (Lev. 19:12). Someone says,
"So help me, God, this is true," then proceeds to tell a deliberate
falsehood. The reinforcement of a lie with the use of God's name
violates the third commandment.

Court oaths are not wrong, though some doubt their propriety.
To hear God's name slurred over in court makes some object to
oaths. But if one really must call God to witness to the truth, he
is not at fault.

Oaths were common in both Old and New Testaments. Abraham
made Eliezer, his steward, promise with an oath not to take a
daughter of the Canaanites for Isaac's wife (Gen. 24:2-3). "The
Lord do so to me, and more also," were the words on Ruth's lips
in pledging loyalty to her mother-in-law (Ruth 1:17). More than
once Paul called God to witness to some weighty utterance
(2 Cor. 1:23; Phil. 1:8). Christ was placed under oath when the
high priest said, "I adjure Thee by the living God that Thou tell us
whether Thou be the Christ" (Matt. 26:63).

An oath can be an act of worship and witness, for it recognizes
God's existence, omniscience, and omnipresence, and admits His

moral government over the world involving accountability of all men to Him as judge. No atheist or skeptic has a right to take such an oath.

By using substitutes for God's name in trivial oaths The Hebrews divided oaths into light and weighty. On unimportant matters they would not invoke God's name, but used substitutes. Since the divine name was omitted, they believed they could break these vows with impunity. But Jesus condemned this practice, teaching that you can't keep God out of *any* promise or transaction. He's everywhere present whether His name is intoned or not. Referring to some of these substitutes for God's name, Jesus said, "Swear not at all; neither by heaven, for it is God's throne; nor by the earth, for it is His footstool; neither by Jerusalem, for it is the city of the great King. Neither shalt thou swear by thy head, because thou canst not make one hair white or black" (Matt. 5:34-36).

Because God is everywhere, whether His name is mentioned or not, all promises are made in His presence. An unadorned *yes* is all that is ordinarily necessary. Jesus concluded, "Let your communication be, 'Yea, yea; Nay, nay,' for whatsoever is more than these cometh of evil" (Matt. 5:37).

By imploring God's name to some unworthy end How often we hear someone in a moment of temper exclaim, "God damn him!" Sometimes the utterer really means it, but usually he has merely introduced God's name as a vent for anger. He has irreverently asked God to do something unworthy of Himself, for God does not damn arbitrarily.

Foolish vows drag down God's name. Jephthah swore, if victorious in battle, to offer as a burnt offering whoever first came out of his house to greet him. Little did he realize that his only daughter would be the one (Judges 11:30-40). King Saul foolishly vowed a curse on any man eating food before evening on a day of battle (1 Sam. 14:24). His own son Jonathan didn't hear the curse and ate, but his life was spared by the people.

Satan misused the name of God when he tempted Christ to jump from the temple pinnacle. He misquoted a promise from the Psalms which included a reference to God. To involve the divine name as a guarantee of protection while engaging in a foolish stunt would be to tempt God according to Jesus' answer (Matt. 4:6-7). To ask God to protect you as you needlessly drive 80 miles an hour down a 55-mile-speed-limit road is to appropriate God's name for an unworthy end.

When we use God's name to reinforce our opinions, claiming to know how God reacts to certain situations on which we have strong feelings, such as claiming God to be for the pacifist, total abstainer, or vegetarian, is to use His name lightly. Annoyed parents who threaten their children with "God will punish you" may be using His name in vain.

By using God's name unthinkingly in worship   Someone said that God's name is taken in vain more times in church than anywhere else. Needless repetition—the introduction of God's name or some form of it too frequently and needlessly—borders on vain use.

So does singing God's name without proper respect or concentration. Do we sing His praises without contemplating His worth? Do we make promises to Him in hymns without thinking of what we are pledging?

It's possible to use God's name lightly in prayer. The one who prays for health or deliverance while seriously sick or in desperate danger, and then reneges on the promises made in the hour of need, is guilty of violating the third commandment.

When we thank God for food, then use the resultant strength in dissipation, we've used God's name emptily. When someone prays, "God bless my business," then indulges in crooked commercial practices, God's name has been used wastefully. If we pray "in Christ's name" when it's really for our own sake, prayer has become a fireside chat with deity in which we merely ask for a blanket endorsement for our plans and interests, using Christ's name in vain.

Even in the judgment day some will use that name in vain, saying, "Lord, Lord." The answer will come, "I never knew you: depart from Me" (Matt. 7:21, 23).

By using God's name as gap-fillers in conversation   Little Mary, attending Sunday School for the first time one Christmas season, eagerly listened as her teacher told of the birth of the Saviour. She thrilled to the story of the angels, the wise men, the star, and the gifts. Then the teacher added, "And they called His name *Jesus.*"

"Why did they have to name such a sweet Baby a swear word?" Mary exclaimed. It was the first time Mary had ever heard the name of Jesus except in swearing.

The careless use of God's name in conversation is all too common. If the devil incarnate belched out blasphemy in our hearing, we would probably recoil. Likewise, our ears ought to tingle to hear that divine name used flippantly in every other sentence by thoughtless people.

Often when swear words are removed from conversation, little of importance remains. A policeman was asked by a judge what the prisoner said when arrested. "Leaving out the bad language," replied the officer, "not a word." Too often swearing is a pointless verbal habit that displaces any serious reference to the Almighty.

A casual reading of even the finest prose and poetry shows how prone men are to drag profanity into the most trivial of affairs. In moments of surprise people exclaim, "My God!" "Good God!" "Oh Lord!" God's name is degraded to the status of an exclamation point!

When someone sneezes, another may react with "God bless you!" If the heart at that moment genuinely desires God's blessing, well and good, but if not, God's name is used carelessly.

To a question the reply may be given, "Only God Almighty knows." Such an answer could be an honest reference to divine omniscience. Too often, however, it is just a flippant retort.

Many slang expressions are substitutions for or variations of powerful swearwords.

For centuries Englishmen have been famed for the forthrightness and frequency of their oaths. "By the splendor of God" was William the Conqueror's favorite oath. Henry II swore by God's eyes. Another by God's tooth.

So impressive were some medieval swearers that their children inherited names that memorialized their profane art. Some surnames in English history are *Godbode, God-me-fetch,* and *Godsowl.* The favorite name the French gave the Englishman in their plays was *John Goddano.*

Servants in medieval England could swear profusely but never with the variety and delicacy of their masters. Gentlemen seldom opened their mouths without calling on their Creator to curse, sink, confound, or blast them.

Then, as time went on, favorite oaths were shortened and stereotyped. Today these swearwords are used in abbreviated form by people who do not realize what terrible oaths they are employing. Professors of languages inform us that "By God's wounds" became *zounds,* "God's blood" became *adsblud,* "Jehovah" became *by Jove,* "God" became *by gad,* "By golly" became *by gum.* For "Jesus" the following forms developed—*gee whiz, jeeze, Jerusalem, gee,* and *gee whillikins.* Instead of "Christ" came *cripes, Jiminy Christmas, jeepers creepers,* and *for crying out loud.* "Lord" gave way to "Lawdy" and "law sakes" (*The Roving Bible,* Lawrence E. Nelson, Abingdon-Cokesbury, N.Y.).

It has been suggested that "gee" is merely the first letter of *God* and the first syllable of *Jesus*—a coward's way of swearing? "Gosh" is *God* with the final letter shaded into a slush as though reluctant to utter it. "Godamighty" is a slurred *God Almighty,* while "Doggone it" and "darn it" are but a play on *God damn it.*

Perhaps you protest, "I say these words but I don't mean anything by it." That's just the point. That's exactly what the third commandment forbids. It could be paraphrased, "Thou shalt not take the name of the Lord without meaning something by it."

Swearing Is Foolish

In Chaucer's *Canterbury Tales,* as the pilgrims journeyed toward Canterbury, they thoughtlessly invoked all the saints in the calendar. Even though headed for a sacred destination, they swore by Christ and His body and His wounds, till the "For God's bones" and "By God's dignity" drove the parson to protest, "What aileth the man so sinfully to swear?" He asked a question that baffles full explanation. Especially puzzling is why should man use words that involve deity?

How man falls into the habit is understandable. Ruffled by some momentary excitement, the mind seeks a safety valve. It seizes on expressions which the person has heard others utter in moments of emotional strain. After giving vent to one's feelings with swear words a few times, it becomes facile and second nature. Then it may be indulged even when the mind is undisturbed and unruffled.

When Branch Rickey was manager of the Brooklyn Dodgers, he was at a meeting negotiating a contract for pro football at Ebbets Field. Suddenly, throwing down his pencil, Rickey growled, "The deal's off." When the others asked why, he replied, "Because you've been talking about a Friend of mine, and I don't like it."

Bewildered, they protested they hadn't been talking about any friend of his. They were enlightened when Ricky reminded them of their constant profane use of the name of Jesus Christ. The men apologized and negotiations continued.

Swearing is pointless. If some profit accrued from swearing, we might understand the practice. "Ten Reasons Why I Swear" is the arresting title of a tract distributed by Alex Dunlap, which throws into clear relief the foolishness of the habit.

1. It pleases mother so much.
2. It is a fine mark of manliness.
3. It proves I have self-control.
4. It indicates how clearly my mind operates.
5. It makes my conversation so pleasing to everybody.
6. It leaves no doubt in anyone's mind as to my good breeding.
7. It impresses people that I have more than an ordinary education.
8. It is an unmistakable sign of culture and refinement.
9. It makes me a very desirable personality among women and children and respectable society.
10. It is my way of honoring God, who said, "Thou shalt not take the name of the Lord thy God in vain."

When we consider that Jesus Christ came from heaven to shed His blood for us, it is bewildering that anyone should use that name in profanity. A man who had just used Christ's name many times as a swearword was asked, "Why don't you try your mother's name?" We would never speak disparagingly of a loving mother. Why speak flippantly of Christ whose love exceeds that of the fondest mother?

Swearing is neither smart, sensible, nor worthwhile. A traveling salesman was asked, "Are you paid anything for swearing?"

His answer was no.

"You certainly work cheap!" exclaimed the other. "You lay aside your character as a gentleman, inflict pain on your friends, break a commandment, lose your own soul, and all for nothing!"

Swearing is poisonous. In England a nobleman came to visit the Wedgwood factory, famous for pottery, and was shown around by a lad aged 15. Mr. Wedgwood followed a few steps behind. During the tour the English peer, a recklessly irreverent man though a brilliant conversationalist, shocked, then captivated the lad, who began to laugh heartily at his profanity. When the tour was over, Mr. Wedgwood sat in his office with the nobleman. Holding a beautiful vase before the peer, who was about to receive it, Mr. Wedgwood deliberately dropped it on the floor shattering it in countless pieces. Angrily the peer demanded, "Why did you do that?"

"There are things more precious than this piece of pottery," said Mr. Wedgwood. "Sir, I can make another vase as beautiful as this, but you cannot give back that boy his former simple reverence which you have destroyed with your irreverent talk!"

When children, too young to know the meaning of the words they utter, hurl blasphemous oaths at each other at play, why should adults be shocked if they are only hearing their own language come home?

Said the poet Cowper:

> It chills my blood to hear the blest Supreme
> Rudely appealed to on each trifling theme!
> Maintain your rank; vulgarity despise;
> To swear is neither brave, polite, nor wise.
> You would not swear upon the bed of death;
> Reflect! Your Maker now could stop your breath!

God's Name to Be Honored

Following the rule of interpretation which says that negative commands should be restated positively, we formulate the third commandment thus, "Thou shalt honor the name of the Lord thy God." To help us do so, here are some brief suggestions:

1. Recall that speech is a marvelous gift of God. Speech is one of the ways man is differentiated from animals. Made in the image of God, man is a thinking creature. Because man can think, God has also given him the ability to express his thoughts in speech. So God has placed in man a highly developed voice box which permits the articulation of involved linguistic sounds. Animals make distinctive sounds—barking, meowing, oinking—and even get limited messages to each other, but they cannot communicate by speech. How wrong to abuse this wonderful gift by speaking God's name in vain.

2. Remember that swearing needs forgiveness. A sergeant in charge of a mess hall during World War II, concerned over the swearing there, devised a plan. He took a quart fruit jar, sealed it, cut a slot in the lid, and labeled it, "Swear can—5¢ for each swearword." *But five cents cannot atone for taking God's name in vain.* Swearing is so serious it took the death of Christ to provide forgiveness. If swearing had been the only sin, Jesus Christ would still have had to die.

3. Recognize that the source of trouble lies deeper than the tongue. Mothers sometimes warn their children, "If you don't stop your bad language, I'll wash your mouth out with soap." Washing the mouth out with soap may curb the practice but it won't cure the cause of swearing. The root of the trouble lies deeper—in the heart. It takes the regenerating power of Christ to transform the moral base and give new motivation.

During the Welsh revival in the early part of this century many miners had to get new pit ponies. The converts had such a radical change of vocabulary that the ponies would not respond to their new non-blasphemous commands.

4. Beware of all substitutes in swearing. Examine your exclamations in moments of surprise. Ask a friend to point out any expressions in conversation which are in reality just variations of swearwords. Then appropriate the power of the indwelling Spirit to stop using them. Strive more earnestly than if trying to correct some grammatical mistake of which you were frequently guilty.

5. Suppress all inordinate anger. Anger easily gives way to unkind words and mean deeds. Most frequent among unkind words are expressions involving God's name. Ask God for self-control. "Be ye angry and sin not" (Eph. 4:26).

6. Cultivate a sense of reverence at the name of God. Whenever we speak the divine name, we should think who God is—the only true God, omnipotent, omnipresent, omniscient, unchangeable, independent, holy, righteous, just, loving. Think of what God has done—His watchcare, providence, and above all, His gift of Christ. Think of what Christ has suffered on our behalf. Respect and awe for the divine name will grow, making it difficult if not impossible to use it frivolously.

On the other hand, irreverent use of God's name unconsciously cuts the connection with God, virtually denies the existence of anything beyond the human, subconsciously scars sensitivity to spiritual reality, and tends to cancel awareness of the holy. "The name of the Lord is a strong tower; the righteous runneth into it, and is safe" (Prov. 18:10). But careless use of that name has a deadening effect, sapping strength from that which is meant to be a strong tower. Thus the swearer will find it difficult in time of need, even embarrassing, to implore God's mercy and help.

Cultivate a sense of God's presence. If we were in the presence of some earthly potentate, we would not misuse his name. By remembering we are always in God's presence, we shall be careful how we use His name. It is said that Sir Isaac Newton never mentioned God in conversation without visible pause, and if his head were covered at the time, he raised his hat.

A missionary to the Orient tells how a 20-year-old lad approached a temple, removed his sandals, and bowed before the idol. Drawing a dagger from beneath his shirt, in one quick swipe he cut off his tongue and offered it to the silent, lifeless image. In minutes he lay unconscious in a pool of blood at the feet of the statue. Hundreds of people soon gathered as the news of the sacrifice spread. Later he was taken to the hospital, where he recovered. God wants our tongues, not cut off in homage to some false god, but dedicated to the worship and service of the one true God.

We need to keep praying, "Hallowed be Thy name" till that day when every knee shall bow and every tongue shall confess that name which is above every name—Jesus.

5

What About Sunday?

Commandment Four: "Remember the Sabbath Day, to keep it holy" (Ex. 20:8).

John D. Rockefeller, founding father of the millionaire family dynasty, loved ice-skating. Yet he would never skate on Sunday or let workmen flood his yard till a minute after midnight Monday morning. His wife even served cold meals on Sundays because cooking was considered a sin.

Two generations later, a commentator in the 1960s remarked, "It takes real application to get through the mammoth *New York Times,* attend church, play 18 holes of golf, catch the second game of a TV doubleheader, pick up the Ed Sullivan Show, grab a late snack before getting a good night's sleep in preparation for a fruitful Monday."

Noting such radical change in Sunday observance led someone to remark, "Our great-grandfathers called it the Holy Sabbath; our grandfathers, the Sabbath; our fathers, Sunday; but today we call it the weekend. And many think it is getting weaker all the time."

A book, *The Weekenders,* reported the various stimulating ways people spend their weekends, then urged the enrichment of life through wise and innovative use of weekend time. One serious omission stood out amidst all the suggestions—no mention of church or worship.

Longest of all the commandments, the fourth reads, "Remember the Sabbath Day, to keep it holy. Six days shalt thou labor, and do all thy work: But the seventh day is the Sabbath of the Lord thy God: in it thou shalt not do any work, thou, nor thy son, nor thy daughter, thy manservant, nor thy maidservant, nor thy cattle, nor thy stranger that is within thy gates: For in six days the Lord made heaven and earth, the sea, and all that in them is, and rested the seventh day: wherefore the Lord blessed the Sabbath Day, and hallowed it" (Ex. 20:8-11).

The institution of the Sabbath can be traced back to creation, before any act of human history occurred (Gen. 2:1-3). Because no other mention is made till the giving of the law at Sinai, many believe the Sabbath was not observed till then. Others point out that the argument from silence is inconclusive and that the Sabbath was later observed for over 500 years without mention (from Deut. 5:15 to 2 Kings 4:23). Also, since the word *remember* seems to point back in time, some Bible teachers believe Sabbath observance was part of creation ethics, binding on man from the beginning.

Answers to this and other knotty questions about the Sabbath-Sunday problem are neither easy nor unanimous.

- Is the command to keep the Sabbath binding today?
- Why do most Christians keep Sunday instead of Saturday?
- How should we observe the day? What may or may not be done?
- Or is every day the same with no special observance needed?

Is the Sabbath Binding Today?

Is the fourth commandment binding on New Testament believers today? The answer is a paradoxical no and yes. The Synod of Dort in 1619 said, "In the fourth commandment of the Law of God there is something ceremonial, and something moral. The resting upon the seventh day after creation and the strict observance of it, which was particularly imposed upon Jewish people, was a ceremonial part of that law. But the moral part is, that a certain day be fixed and appropriated to the service and the holy meditation upon Him." A similar concept was stated in the Westminster Confession, first published in 1647.

These statements acknowledge a continuing principle in the fourth commandment proper for today's believers. Dr. Nelson

Bell wrote in *Christianity Today,* "The Ten Commandments have never been abrogated. It is still wrong to kill, to steal, to commit adultery. . . . To deny the validity of one day in seven as a day of rest and spiritual refreshment is to miss one of God's greatest gifts to mankind." To rule out completely one of the Ten Commandments from the practice of the New Testament, while the other nine are repeated in it, seems to fragment the Decalogue.

But we do emphasize that the ceremonial aspect of this commandment is annulled. The Sabbath was something special, a sign, between God and Israel (Ex. 31:16-17). The New Testament, after Pentecost, never enjoins the observance of the Sabbath. The list of items required of Gentile converts by the Jerusalem Council, which dealt with the relationship of Gentile Christians to the law of Moses, contained no reference to Sabbath-keeping. It is noteworthy that not only does no verse in any New Testament epistle command Sabbath-keeping, but also Sabbath-breaking is never included in any list of sins in any of the epistles. Violations of all other of the nine commandments are spelled out as sins, but Sabbath-breaking is omitted.

Of the nine post-Pentecost references to the seventh-day Sabbath, eight speak not of a Christian gathering, but of a strictly Jewish service, which Paul attended for the purpose of evangelizing (Acts 13:14, 27, 42, 44; 15:21; 16:13; 17:2; 18:4). The ninth reference declares the Christian's liberty from Sabbath law. In the Colossian church one group, who combined incipient Gnosticism with Jewish legalism, contended for a Christian observance of the Sabbath. Paul repudiated this claim in rather plain language: "Let no man therefore judge you in meat, or in drink, or in respect of an holyday, or of the new moon, or of the sabbath days" (Col. 2:16). In the Galatian epistle Paul rebuked the observance of "days, and months, and times, and years" as the error of returning to weak, beggarly, and enslaving elements (4:9-10).

To sum up: the ceremonial, seventh-day aspect of the fourth commandment is no longer binding on believers. But the principle of devoting time to God still continues.

Why Do We Keep Sunday?

The first day of the week receives unusual emphasis in the New

Testament. All four Gospels record the resurrection on the first day (Matt. 28:1; Mark 16:2; Luke 24:1; John 20:1, 19). On the following Sunday, Jesus appeared to Thomas. No other event recorded in the four Gospels is so connected with a definite day as the resurrection of Christ. So it's not surprising that on the first day of the week the disciples gathered to commemorate their Master's resurrection.

Paul instructed the Corinthians about their offering for the poor at Jerusalem as follows: "Upon the first day of the week let every one of you lay by him in store, as God hath prospered him." The inescapable interpretation is that they were to bring their funds when they met each first day for worship (1 Cor. 16:1-2). Similar advice was given other churches.

En route to Jerusalem on his third missionary journey, Paul met with the disciples at Troas for worship, instruction, and the Lord's Supper on the first day of the week. The verb *came together* (Acts 20:7) is the common word for assembling in church meetings, and gives us our English word *synagogue*. Among those assembled were converted Jews, who formerly "synagogued" on Saturday, but who now "synagogued" on Sunday. Though Paul was there for seven days, no mention is made of any service on Saturday, but the first-day gathering is reported and is seemingly normative.

The first day of the week is called "the Lord's Day" by the Apostle John. It is not "the day of the Lord" referring to the end of time, but rather the adjective "lordly" or "imperial." The last living disciple, John the Beloved, banished to the desolate isle of Patmos, was meditating on spiritual matters on the first day of the week when he was given a vision of his glorified Master. He reports, "I was in the spirit on the Lord's Day" (Rev. 1:10). Also, Pentecost, the day the Holy Spirit was given, fell on the first day of the week, and is observed today as the seventh Sunday after Easter.

Ample documentary evidence indicates that the early Church observed the first day of the week. Ignatius, writing around A.D. 107 to the Magnesians, said, "They who walked in ancient customs came to a new hope, no longer living for the Sabbath, but for the Lord's Day, on which also our Light arose" (chap. 9).

Another early post-apostolic letter, the Epistle of Barnabas, dated not later than A.D. 130, stated, "We also celebrate with gladness the eighth day, whereon indeed Jesus rose from the dead" (15:9). When Emperor Constantine in the fourth century declared Sunday the day to be observed, he was only putting official approval on a day which had already been set aside for some 300 years.

Are We Commanded to Observe Sunday as Our Sabbath?

Both the Synod of Dort and the Westminster Confession of Faith affirm that the seventh-day Sabbath was changed to the first day, the Lord's Day, in the New Testament dispensation. They hold that Sunday is now the Sabbath for the Christian.

However, historically, Christendom has not been united on this subject. Martin Luther said, "We Christians . . . have the liberty to turn Monday or some other day of the week into Sunday if the Sabbath or Sunday does not please us" (sermon on Oct. 5, 1544). Luther doubtless had in mind Paul's remarks, "One man esteemeth one day above another: another esteemeth every day alike. Let every man be fully persuaded in his own mind" (Rom. 14:5). Paul seems to say that the believer has liberty to observe any day he chooses.

Calvin was equally clear in holding that though men and maids should have a day for rest and worship, the day was not fixed as it was for the Jews. He said, "The observance of days among us is a free service and void of all superstition" (*Institutes,* 2.8.34).

The position of the Reformers was this. They refused to identify the Lord's Day as the Sabbath. On the other hand, they saw that total freedom to observe any day could lead to keeping no day. Thus, many of them realized the need for denoting a particular day, thereby preserving order, reverence, decency, and peace in the church. Because Christ rose on Sunday and because that day had been almost universally adopted from apostolic times, Sunday was generally observed. But the day was a voluntary observance, not a matter of biblical coercion.

Both views are held by the church today. Some hold that Sunday is now the Sabbath. Others believe that Sunday is not the Sabbath but the expedient and proper day to keep voluntarily.

The common denominator of both views is that Sunday is special. A Scofield Reference Bible note (under Matt. 12:1) reads, "The Christian first day perpetuates in the dispensation of grace the principle that one-seventh of the time is especially sacred, but in all other respects is in contrast with the Sabbath."

How Should Sunday Be Observed?

Know how the word *sundae* came to be? Around 1875 the city fathers of Evanston, Ill. passed a law forbidding the sale of ice cream sodas on Sunday. Someone thought of serving ice cream with syrup but no soda water. This Sunday delicacy became quite popular, so that on weekdays many asked for Sundays. City officials objected to naming the dish after the holy day, so changed the spelling. Sundae it has been ever since.

Strict regulations regarding Sunday conduct (often called Blue Laws) remind us of the endless rules of the Pharisees of Jesus' day for Sabbath observance. Some 1,521 things were not permissible on the day, including rescuing a drowning person. If a man were bitten by a flea on the Sabbath, he was to permit the flea to keep on biting, for trying to counter the flea would make the man guilty of the sin of hunting on the Sabbath. Untying knots which needed only one hand for unraveling was permissible, but if two hands were required, this was work and forbidden. Our Lord found Himself repeatedly in conflict with the Pharisees over His failure to obey their strictures.

In later centuries Sunday sabbatarians drew up as detailed a list of prohibitions as ever did the Pharisees. Some people would not sweep or dust the house, make the beds, or allow any food to be cooked on Sunday. In Scotland in the 17th century, one poor fellow was hailed into court for smiling on the Sabbath. Jonathan Edwards once resolved never to utter anything humorous on the Lord's Day. One family was obliged to eat pancakes that had been made on Saturday.

Those who want to remove the *bath* from sabbath and the *sun* from Sunday are often inconsistent. A missionary was rebuked by his hostess for typing correspondence on Sunday; later he found her penning a letter. On a visit to the Holy Land, Dr. Wilbur Smith asked a Hebrew scholar for his autograph. The scholar refused, for writing two consecutive words was not permissible on the Sabbath. Moments later in the heat of argument the Hebrew scholar climbed three rungs of a ladder to the eighth shelf of his library to reach a book to reinforce a point of discussion.

Such attitudes cannot be supported from the Bible. In fact, when it comes to Sunday, the New Testament is silent on what may not be done. Perhaps a better approach would be to ask what is right to do on Sunday. Spending our time profitably would leave little time for questionable things. However we spend the day, it should not be construed as keeping the Old Testament Sabbath but as consistent with the continuing principle of the fourth commandment to devote some time regularly to the Lord.

Here are some suggestions.

Rest   Someone said, "The best insurance against car accidents is a Sunday afternoon nap."

Sabbath means "rest." Physical rest was required by the fourth commandment, "In it thou shalt not do any work" (Ex. 20:8, 10). Rest in a spiritual sense is also implicit in the Lord's Day, because the resurrection brought the stamp of divine approval on Christ's finished work in which we rest (Heb. 4:8-11).

Nothing indicates that work was suspended on the Lord's Day during the early years of the church. Slaves, who composed much of the church membership, had no choice but to work. As time went by, according to historians, the Christian community moved toward the suspension of ordinary activities on Sunday. This tendency found official support in Constantine's edict ordering all work to stop in the cities on the Lord's Day. He permitted agricultural work to continue lest crops be ruined.

Sunday closing of businesses, observed by much of the general community today, is mainly on humanitarian grounds. Physically we need a change, for a rundown person is an unproductive person. Admittedly, some jobs have to be done on Sunday. But where possible the believer should abstain from the common and servile tasks of life, whether employed by others or at home. Works of necessity and piety may be done. Jesus' disciples plucked corn on the Sabbath (Matt. 12:1-8).

However, rest need not be equated with inactivity. The burdensome labor of earlier generations made the need for sheer physical rest on Sunday more acute than today. Now, with many occupations not physically demanding, relaxation might be better secured by mildly active, noncompetitive recreation. So where do we draw the line? It's hard to understand how enduring the frustrations of jammed highways to drive to and from a huge stadium to watch professional athletes perform can be considered rest or recreation. Whatever we do should not return us to work Monday more tired than we came home Friday.

In a day of elastic conscience in the matter of Sunday public sports, we should be reminded that earlier generations held strong convictions. When Eric Liddel, a British record holder for the 100 yards, found out a few months in advance that the heats for the 100 meters in the 1924 Paris Olympic Games would be run on a Sunday, he quietly affirmed, "I'm not running." Instead he trained for the 400 meters. At the Olympics he won, setting a new world's record. He received real encouragement just before the race when a stranger handed him a piece of paper which read, "Them that honor Me I will honor" (1 Sam. 2:30). Eric Liddel later became a missionary, and died in a Japanese internment camp in China in May 1945.

Worship   Once a year, on Easter, we commemorate the resurrection of Christ. However, each Sunday morning should find us meditating on such thoughts as prompted Isaac Watts to write:

> *This is the day when Christ arose*
> *So early from the dead;*
> *Why should I keep my eyelids closed,*
> *And waste my hours in bed?*

On Sundays the Early Church took time to worship, study the Scriptures, fellowship, pray, sing, give, encourage one another, and observe the Lord's Supper. In meeting on the Lord's Day, saints look back to God's finished redemption which has brought spiritual rest. They also look forward to the day when a fallen creation, now groaning, will receive its redemption through the saving work of Christ. On Sundays believers can witness to their contemporaries both what Christ has done and will yet do.

Since we are creatures of eternity as well as of time, since we are to live by every word of God as well as by bread, we need the spiritual sustenance that comes from assembling with other saints. Sunday, above all other days, provides the leisure and opportunity to obey the command to gather for corporate worship (Heb. 10:25). A little boy, asked to define the Lord's Day, replied, "It's a day to get acquainted with God."

The practice of Jesus on His day of rest reveals the priority of worship and sets a worthy example for His followers. "And He came to Nazareth, . . . and, as His custom was, He went into the synagogue on the Sabbath Day" (Luke 4:16).

Contemplation   The Apostle John was apparently meditating on spiritual truth when Christ revealed Himself to him (Rev. 1:10). What better day is there to study the Word, to engage in serious conversation on holy topics, to memorize Bible verses, to start study for next week's Sunday School lesson, to read Christian literature.

The only reading some Christians do that day is the Sunday newspaper. By contrast, one man devoted his Sunday afternoons for over 30 years to compile his own personal concordance to the Bible.

Dr. Frank E. Gaebelein, former headmaster of Stony Brook School, suggests cultural contemplation with discrimination, using Paul's criterion of "whatsoever things are true . . . and lovely" (Phil. 4:8), as fit exercise for a Christian's Sunday. A vesper organ program, piano recital, chamber music, art exhibit, visit to a museum, or some similarly enriching experience would qualify.

Joy   In Judaism a joyous atmosphere was to prevail on the Sabbath. People were to have two complete changes of attire, one for weekdays, but one exclusively for the Sabbath. It was permissible to sleep a little longer on the Sabbath. Knives sharpened in advance would add to the enjoyment of Sabbath food, a larger quantity of which was to be prepared for that day. Jesus socialized on the Sabbath, accepting an invitation to dinner at the home of a Pharisee (Luke 14:1).

Family get-togethers on Sunday bring delight, as sons and daughters return for a meal, permitting grandchildren to get acquainted with their grandparents. Adding to family festiveness, the satisfactions of rest, worship, contemplation, and service should make it, in the words of a hymn, "O day of rest and gladness, O day of joy and light."

Service   Our Lord often healed on the Sabbath and was sometimes severely criticized for it (Mark 1:21-28; Luke 4:31-41; John 5:1-16). Repeatedly He defended doing good on that day. Once the Pharisees didn't want Jesus to heal a man with a withered hand on the holy day. With eyes flashing angrily, He showed them their inconsistency in rescuing a sheep from a pit on the Sabbath while objecting to helping a man whose value far exceeds that of a sheep (Mark 3:5; Matt. 12:9-14). A similar attitude to that of the merciless Pharisees was reflected centuries later in the plight of a family in Glasgow, Scotland. Destitute on the street on a snowy night in January 1847, with one child of seven dead and the mother dying of TB, they learned that the church authorities had ruled that soup kitchens for the destitute were not to be opened on the Sabbath.

The New Testament strongly urges helping others in a practical way. What better way to utilize the free hours of the Lord's Day than to visit the sick, needy, sorrowing, shut-in, nursing homes, or prisons?

In the Lord's Day the child of God has a marvelous possession. Dr. Hudson Armerding, Wheaton College president, commented, "Perhaps the mental and emotional illness that plagues even the Christian community might be lessened if men deliberately set aside the pressures and tensions of demanding schedules and devoted one day in seven to meditation, worship, and fellowship. Like the other nine commandments, the fourth is designed to enable man to serve his Creator better" ("The Lord's Day is not Passé," *Christianity Today*). Sunday is the day that sees us "safely through another week."

If we lose Sunday we lose our finest opportunity to worship God, serve our fellowman, and bring refreshment to ourselves. D. L. Moody said, "Show me a nation that has given up the Sabbath and I will show you a nation that has the seeds of decay."

An elderly lady who worked hard washing floors six mornings a week was on her way to Sunday morning church. A friend who knew how hard she worked asked, "Wouldn't it be better for you to sleep late on Sunday morning? Wouldn't it help you keep going?" The lady leaned back on her heels and exclaimed, "It's going to church on Sunday that keeps me going the other six days of the week!"

Your Sunday may determine your week. More than that, your months, your years, your eternity.

6

Children and Parents

Commandment Five: "Honor thy father and thy mother" (Ex. 20:12).

A Sunday School teacher asked his class to write out the fifth commandment. One lad wrote, "Humor thy father and thy mother." Another penned, "Honor thy pirates." While parents are neither pirates nor need humoring, certain obligations are binding on both children and parents.

The fifth commandment, which reads, "Honor thy father and thy mother," carries a reward for children who keep it: "that thy days be long upon the land which the Lord thy God giveth thee" (Ex. 20:12). Paul comments that this was "the first commandment with promise" (Eph. 6:2). Though today obedience to parents does not bring long life in the land of Cannan, it does bring the blessings that come from following parental instruction. Furthermore, it is the right thing for children to do (Eph. 6:1), and "is well pleasing unto the Lord" (Col. 3:20).

How needed is this commandment in the midst of the spirit of rebellion that pervades society today! Authority is flouted, permissiveness is flaunted. One law school professor said, "We are heading for anarchy in this country." Noted marriage counselor David R. Mace warned, "Revolutionary forces have launched an attack on family life such as we have never before experienced."

The first four commandments deal with duty under God's authority. The fifth turns to the area under man's lordship. Because the first human authority we meet in life is that of parents, the fifth commandment speaks of honor to father and mother.

The Honor Due Parents

An inscription on an old Egyptian tomb read, "We are living in a dying and decadent age. Youth is corrupt, lacking in respect for its elders." Perhaps the fifth commandment has been needed in all ages.

In what does honor to parents consist?

Reverence   Children should respect their parents. Their speech should never be impudent, sharp, contemptible, mocking, despising, or answering with a sassy, "I won't," or referring to parents as "the old man" or "the old woman." The Old Testament was hard on discourtesy to parents. "He that curseth his father or his mother shall surely be put to death" (Ex. 21:17).

Not only speech, but gesture and manner of life should honor parents. No child should sit while mother must stand, stick his tongue out at father, or give either a dirty look. No respectful boy will get the family name smeared in the local paper in disgrace. "Don't tell my mother" is often the cry of a boy who should have thought of his parents before committing the misdeed that get him into trouble with the police.

Children should treat their parents kindly, seek to make them happy, and pray they will never do anything to bring them shame or sorrow, as did Esau when he brought "grief of mind" to his father and mother by marrying a heathen girl (Gen. 26:34-35).

Obedience   Sometimes youth thinks itself wiser than its elders. Someone said, "Young men think old men fools, and old men know young men to be so." Since the years bring increase in wisdom, children should defer to the advice and guidance of parents. One boy admitted how much smarter his folks had become between the time he was 12 and 18. Children should trust that parental love will never command anything but what is for the child's good.

Occasions sometimes arise requiring immediate, unquestioning obedience. A missionary's little boy playing in his yard in the Congo suddenly heard his father's voice. "Son, obey me instantly! Drop on your stomach!" The boy obeyed without a question. "Now crawl toward me as fast as you can!" Again the lad obeyed.

"Now stand up and run to me!" The boy ran to his father's arms. Then he looked back at the tree under which he had been playing. Hanging from a branch was a deadly, 15-foot snake. Suppose the boy had paused to argue, "Why, Dad?" or "Do I have to do it now?"

When given a task, children should do it immediately and gladly, remembering David, who though destined for a throne, tended sheep, the job given the youngest in the family because it was considered most menial. The example of our Lord is significant. At 12 years of age He "went down with them [parents], and came to Nazareth, and was subject unto them" (Luke 2:51).

As long as a son or daughter is single and supported by the parents, that child still owes obedience to them. Many non-Christian parents have been won to Christian faith because a believing child wisely obeyed them. At marriage a new home is established which creates a new seat of authority. But other aspects of honor to parents still pertain. However, when a parent orders a child to do something plainly contrary to the Word of God, the child should gracefully suggest an alternative that does not demand anti-Christian action. In the final analysis, all alternatives exhausted, obedience to God takes priority over obedience to parents.

Remuneration   A little boy expressed concern about his parents. He told how his dad worked hard to provide for all his needs, how his mother slaved around the house, cleaned up after him, took care of him when sick. When asked what he had to worry about, he replied, "I'm afraid they might escape."

Most parents do not expect their children to repay them for all the expense of raising them, but they deserve appreciation. A 10-year-old boy left a bill for his father under the dinner plate. Mother picked it up and read, "For doing chores and cutting wood—$1." Mother left a note for her son at the next meal, "For caring for you for 10 years, feeding and clothing you, and for loving you—nothing."

One day five convicts sat looking at a magazine in a prison library.

"Wish my mother had a home like the one in that ad," said one.

Another took the magazine and flipping the pages, remarked, "That's what I wish my ma had. A car so she could come and see me once in a while."

Then the magazine was passed to Bill. But Bill just sat there, musing. The others thought it strange for they knew his mother didn't have anyone left in the world but him. Finally Bill spoke, "I wish"—his voice sounded as if it were coming from the other side of the wall—"that my mother had a good son."

Working hard at school or business, complimenting parents at opportune times, remembering their birthdays and anniversaries, all these help repay parents. A mother who scrimped to put her son through college was able to attend his graduation. He walked across the platform, received his diploma with high honors, then walked down the aisle. But instead of turning in the designated row, he kept walking down to where she sat unnoticed. The young man threw his arms around her neck, planted a kiss on her furrowed brow, dropped the diploma in her lap, and exclaimed, "Here, Mother, you earned it!"

If parents fall into poverty or illness, children should render financial assistance where possible. Piety begins at home with children giving support to needy parents, for this is "good and acceptable before God" (1 Tim. 5:4). Pharisees of Jesus' day found a way to evade this responsibility. Through a ritual they vowed all their resources to God, but were allowed to use their possessions for themselves. They could say to their parents, "Sorry, we cannot help you for all our assets are dedicated to God." Jesus strongly rebuked the Pharisees for this practice, accusing them of breaking the fifth commandment.

Helping parents may involve bringing them into a son's or daughter's home. If this is impractical, it may mean providing suitable quarters elsewhere, perhaps in a nursing home. But this commandment obligates a child with sufficient resources to see that his parents in old age or weakness do not lack for the necessities of life, or visits from time to time. The Lord Jesus, even in His sufferings on the cross, cared for the needs of His mother by committing her into the care of the Apostle John (John 19:26-27).

Children may reap what they sow in this area of life. A man

in the Orient whose people made the practice of exposing the useless aged in a desolate place to die, one day decided to take his old father and leave him out in the wilds. His little boy asked to go along. As they returned home, the little boy piped up, "Father, I'm glad you brought me along today. For now I know where to take you when you get old and useless."

Imitation in godliness   Children should never make fun of their parents' Christianity. Rather they should follow in their steps and imitate their godliness. "My son, keep thy father's commandment, and forsake not the law of thy mother" (Prov. 6:20). Parents who fulfill their obligation to train up their children in the ways of God have every right to expect them, sooner or later, to follow Christ as Saviour and Lord (Prov. 22:6).

One father, who set a good example in many ways, including ushering down a particular aisle of the church for years, died disappointed without seeing his son become a Christian. Ten years later his son was not only a Christian, but was ushering down the very same aisle, which he did the rest of his life.

Duties of Parents

If parents are to be honored, they must be honorable, worthy of respect, obedience, support, and imitation. Reciprocal obligation on the parents' part is acknowledged by Paul in two epistles, where after urging children to obey parents, he adds, "Fathers, provoke not your children" (Eph. 6:4; Col. 3:21).

What are some principles for rearing children in a Christian manner? One expert on child psychology said before marriage, "I have four good ideas on how to raise children, but I have no children." Ten years later he confided, "I have four children but no ideas." In our day of wide-spread family breakdown and the celebrated generation gap, we need to review the duties of parents.

Provision   Paternal love naturally leads most parents to provide for their offspring. An old Jewish proverb says, "God couldn't be everywhere; so He gave us parents." Parental sacrifice is proverbial. During inspection at a Boy Scout camp the director found a large umbrella hidden in a tiny scout's bedroll. When asked to explain the umbrella's presence since it was not on the list to bring, the tenderfoot countered, "Sir, did you ever have a mother?"

It is hard to believe, but true, that thousands of children are deserted annually in our country. The Bible brands as worse than an infidel any head of house who fails to provide for his family (see 1 Tim. 5:8).

Far-sighted provision would include saving for future education or a rainy day. Such is not laying up treasure on earth, but rather heeding the lesson of the ant which gathers its meat in summer for the winter (Prov. 6:6-8).

Not only should parents provide for physical needs, but they should endeavor to give advantages for mental development. They should take an interest in the child's school work. They should make good books available for cultural growth, as well as opportunities for aesthetic appreciation.

Instruction   Beyond physical and mental needs of their children, parents should also take care of spiritual obligations. As children have a duty to obey, parents have a duty to teach them the ways of God. Every parent should be able to say, "I have taught thee in the way of wisdom; . . . take fast hold of instruction; . . . for she is thy life" (Prov. 4:11, 13). If parents taught their children well, the church's work would be mostly done. This is a failure of many parents. They provide good food, dental treatment, medical exams, good schools, books, music. They raise children like so many prize cattle on the hoof, but neglect to lead them to Jesus Christ as Saviour and Pilot over life's tempestuous sea.

Our matriarchal society delegates most spiritual teaching to mothers, whereas in Bible times the father was responsible for the spiritual education of his children. Today Father reasons, "I bring home the bacon. Wife can take care of the children." Some fathers would choke if they had to speak about the Lord to their children. How far from the biblical injunction for fathers to teach their children God's law at every opportunity! "And these words, which I command thee this day, shall be in thine heart: And thou shalt teach them diligently unto thy children, and thou shalt talk of them when thou sittest in thine house, and when thou walkest by the way, and when thou liest down, and when thou risest up" (Deut. 6:6-7). The Old Testament home was virtually a religious institution (Deut. 6:6-8, 20-25).

The New Testament home is likewise to be a place of spiritual instruction. "And, ye fathers, . . . bring them up in the nurture and admonition of the Lord" (Eph. 6:4). Youngsters should hear or read Bible stories for their age level. Young Timothy from a child knew the Holy Scriptures (2 Tim. 3:15).

Parents can help children discern between good and evil, and between truth and error. Spurgeon's mother used to discourse on major doctrines like regeneration and justification when he was only nine. Luther said, "No one should become a father unless he is able to instruct his children in the Ten Commandments and in the Gospel so that he may bring them up true Christians."

Example A couple reprimanded their little girl and boy for noisy quarreling. They replied, "We aren't quarreling. We're just playing mommy and daddy."

Children are great imitators. When we catch a child in some misdeed, the chances are he learned it from some adult, perhaps a parent. A teacher spoke sternly to little Nancy, "You shouldn't tell lies. Your mother wouldn't like it." Replied the little 9-year-old, "Oh, my mother doesn't care. She does it herself. Last night she told me she would be right in the next room all evening while I slept, but when I peeked through the door I saw a strange lady there. My mother went to her club."

Parental talk must be backed by walk. A 10-year-old boy informed his Sunday School teacher that he was never going to read the Bible again. He explained to his startled teacher, "I know Father talks nicely about the Bible, but he never bothers to read it himself."

Someone said, "We take our children to the circus, but send them to Sunday School." Pre-teen children may go willingly to Sunday School and church, even when parents don't attend, but when they reach adolescence, they won't be fooled. No wonder there's a mass exodus of teen-agers from Sunday School and church.

Late one Saturday night a pair of young people were seriously injured in an auto accident. At the hospital the father learned that both had been drinking. A bottle had been found in the car. On the way home the father raged, "If I could find the person who sold these kids that whiskey, I'd kill him!" Going to his cabinet where he kept his liquor, the father found a note in his daughter's handwriting, "Dear Dad, we hope you won't mind us taking your whiskey with us tonight."

Communication   Parents should always assure their children of their love, give them encouragement, welcome their friends, keep the channel of communication open with sympathetic understanding, and spend time with them.

A young man was about to be sentenced for forgery. The judge had known him from childhood, for the boy's father had been a famous legal expert and author of a work titled, "Law of Trusts." The judge asked if the boy remembered his father, whom he had now disgraced. Came the reply, "I remember him perfectly. When I went to him for advice or companionship, he would look up from his manuscript and say, 'Run away, I'm busy.' My father finished his book, and here am I."

Discipline   Someone said, "When a youth begins to sow wild oats, it's time for the father to start the threshing machine." Whether parents resort to giving a pat on the back, low enough, hard enough, and often enough, or use a non-physical approach, the Bible clearly demands the discipline of youth. "He that spareth his rod hateth his son; but he that loveth him chasteneth him betimes" (Prov. 13:24).

Every child is born with a will of his own. The delicate duty of parents is to train that child to obey authority, curbing his will without marring initiative or personality. Parents are responsible for checking the sinful tendencies of their offspring. The sacrilege and adultery committed by Eli's sons at the doors of the tabernacle were blamed on their father's failure. "His sons made themselves vile, and he [Eli] restrained them not" (1 Sam. 3:13).

Overstrictness is just as wrong as overleniency. Paul commanded, "And ye fathers, provoke not your children to wrath" (Eph. 6:4). If our forefathers were guilty of rigidity, the last generation has swung to permissiveness, producing a crop of youth with minimal respect for authority. "In sparing the rod, we raised a beat generation."

When a little boy climbed on a hobby horse in a department

store and refused to get off for his mother and for a clerk despite promises of candy and toys, the store Santa Claus came along and whispered in his ear. Like a shot the lad leaped off the horse and hurried out of the store with his harried mother following close behind. The surprised clerk asked the Santa Claus what he promised him. Came Santa's reply, "I promised him nothing. I told him to get off or I'd kick him right out of his trousers!"

Psychologists tell us that a child, for proper emotional growth, needs the structure of discipline to balance permissiveness. Children, like flowers, should not be stunted by mistreatment nor allowed to grow wild.

Prayer   Job rose early in the morning to ask God's blessing on his children (1:1-5). Hannah not only prayed for a son, but gave Samuel back to God in prayer (1 Sam. 1:11, 26-28). No wonder Samuel became spiritually significant, last of the judges, first of the prophets. Thousands of Christian workers can trace their position of spiritual leadership to praying parents.

In fact, after parents have done their best, providing, teaching, showing, loving, and disciplining, and their heart skips a beat in the face of devilish allurements and pitfalls that surround their children, prayer will be their only resort.

Wider Application

In its broadest sense, the fifth commandment could be stated, "Obey authority." Because the first authority a child meets in life is parents, the command is particularized, "Honor thy father and thy mother." But following the rule of interpretation that a commandment is often stated as a specific of a wider area of ethics, the Puritans regularly expanded this commandment to include several other relationships involving authority—husbands and wives, masters and servants, rulers and subjects, teachers and pupils, and pastor and flock. In both the Ephesian and Colossian epistles, Paul discusses the duties of children and parents in the context of those of wives and husbands, and servants and masters.

A 15-year-old boy, born in London in 1616, lost his parents through the plague. Then he ran away from his master to whom he had been apprenticed by relatives. Wandering aimlessly through the city, he saw people going into church and followed. The sermon, on the fifth commandment, included the duties of servants to masters, and led to his conversion and return to his master. He became a wealthy merchant, using his funds freely in evangelistic work. His name, William Kiffen, was affixed as one of the signers to the famous 1644 London Baptist Confession of Faith.

It's logical for the fifth commandment to deal with a child's duty to parents, for if a child learns to respect this first authority he faces in life, then he is more likely to obey later authorities. Luther said, "What is a city but a collection of houses? Where father and mother rule badly, and let children have their own way, there neither city, town, village, district, kingdom, nor empire can be well and peacefully governed." Paraphrasing Paul, "Obey government. When you disobey government, you disobey God" (see Rom. 13:1-2).

Admittedly, when obedience to God conflicts with duty to parent, country, teacher, or employer, duty to God takes precedence over human authority. Peter and John, ordered by the Sanhedrin not to speak in the name of Jesus, declared their intent to obey God, not the rulers (Acts 4:18-20). But where no conflict arises, the Christian is obligated to respect authority.

How important for parents to teach this respect to their children! For the child who honors parents will more readily respect his teachers, obey the laws of the land, defer to his employer, and *obey the Gospel*. The implications involve not only this life but the life to come.

A lady was asked if she did any literary work. "Oh yes," she replied, "my husband and I are co-authoring three books. Their titles are: Mary, John, and William. They're our three children. Together we're writing their lives."

7

Blood on Our Hands

Commandment Six: "Thou shalt not kill" (Ex. 20:13).

Billboards displaying in bold letters "Thou shalt not kill" went up all over New Orleans in 1974. Because of a runaway homicide rate—over 100 murders the first few months of the year—city fathers wanted to remind citizens of the sixth commandment (Ex. 20:13). Baltimore, another city with a growing homicide problem, offered a $50 bounty for every firearm turned in.

A Chicago periodical pointed out in late 1974 that its city had just passed through an especially tragic weekend. No fewer than 22 persons were shot and killed from suppertime Friday till Monday morning in individual acts of violence, most in robbery attempts. Among the victims was an outstanding Christian leader in Sunday School administration. No riots were involved. Seventy-six others were shot and wounded during the same few hours, and 16 were stabbed in skirmishes which might well have ended in fatalities. Three more lives were rubbed out in neighboring suburbs. All this occurred in a single urban area in a 60-hour span.

FBI crime reports indicated that while Chicago's record is high, some other areas are as bad or worse. Actually, Atlanta ranks first among large American cities in per capita murders, and Detroit is second. No fewer than 19,510 murders were listed across the nation in 1973, an average of more than one each 30 minutes.

How needful in our violent day to emphasize the sanctity of human life. In fact, each of the final six commandments safeguards some aspect of human relationships. While the first four commandments elaborate our love to God, the last six zero in on our duties to fellowmen in the following areas:

Commandment	Protects
5th—obedience	—proper authority
6th—no murder	—neighbor's life
7th—no adultery	—neighbor's marriage
8th—no stealing	—neighbor's property
9th—no lying	—neighbor's reputation
10th—no coveting	—everything pertaining to one's neighbor by requiring proper inner attitude that leads to such honor

All Killing Is Not Murder

Hebrew, like English, has different words for *kill* and *murder*. Most modern versions more accurately render the sixth commandment, "Thou shalt not murder." Not all life-taking is murder.

Animals   Animals may be killed for food. God said to Noah, "Every moving thing that liveth shall be meat for you" (Gen. 9:3). Paul said virtually the same thing (1 Tim. 4:4). Jesus ate fish. Any mad dog or prowling beast endangering human life may be shot. Of course, cruelty to animals should never be tolerated (Prov. 12:10). But murder involves the taking of human life only.

Accidents   The Old Testament made a distinction between accidental and willful killing. Six cities of refuge were conveniently located to which any slayer could flee. If a slaying was intentional, the murderer was put to death. If accidental, such as an axe flying off the handle and fatally striking another, the slayer was granted sanctuary in the city of refuge because he had not plotted the death of his neighbor. Modern law also distinguishes between manslaughter and murder. Murder involves willfulness, a certain degree of premeditation.

Self-defense The Mosaic law justified life-taking if necessary for self-defense. If someone made forcible entry into a house at night, the owner was justified in resisting even to the point of killing the intruder. No action was to be taken against him. This principle, found in both Roman and English law, rests on the premise that those who break into a house by night most likely have murderous intent toward anyone who would thwart them (Ex. 22:2-3).

Capital punishment The oldest record of a murder trial dates back nearly 4,000 years. A two-by-four foot clay tablet found in Iraq in 1950 describes how three men killed another. Brought before the king, the three men along with the victim's wife were tried for murder. The wife was declared innocent, but the three men were executed. This was in 1850 B.C.

From early times the basic law of a life for a life has been followed by nations everywhere. Today controversy revolves around the question of capital punishment. Some claim it was divinely instituted and is socially essential; others label it savage and unchristian. G. Campbell Morgan, well-known Bible expositor, says that in this Christian era, "capital punishment has no place" (*The Ten Commandments,* Revell, Old Tappan, N.J.).

Is it ever morally right to take the life of a murderer? Several Bible passages teach capital punishment for the heinous sin of taking another's life. A few chapters into the Bible is this divine directive, "Whoso sheddeth man's blood, by man shall his blood be shed; for in the image of God made He man" (Gen. 9:6). The Mosaic law broadened the grounds for which a person could be put to death to include adultery, witchcraft, incest, filial rebellion, and kidnapping (Lev. 20:10; Ex. 22:18; Lev. 18:6-18; Deut. 21:18-21; Ex. 21:16). The New Testament presupposes the same basic position as the Old for punishing murderers. Paul declared that the ruler "beareth not the sword in vain; for he is the minister of God, a revenger to execute wrath upon him that doeth evil" (Rom. 13:4).

Wherever possible, criminals should be reformed. But in the case of a murderer, the biblical penalty for taking a human life was loss of one's own life. Justice was the prime basis for capital punishment. The worth of an individual is so great that the supreme penalty is pronounced on anyone who extinguishes another's life.

Many objections against capital punishment are based on abuse and miscarriage of justice: only a small percentage of murderers are found guilty; by far the majority of those who walk that last mile to the death chamber have been poor and friendless; the rich go free through the services of high-priced lawyers; innocent men have gone to the chair.

Floyd Hamilton, the FBI's Public Enemy No. 1 in 1938, today a born-again, witnessing Christian, has definite views on capital punishment because of his brush with the electric chair on a false charge. Hamilton, "the last of the Bonnie and Clyde gang," received sentences totaling 115 years. He served 28 years in prison, 12 of them in Alcatraz. For three years he was in solitary confinement next to "the birdman of Alcatraz." Hamilton was pardoned by the president of the U.S. and the governor of Texas after his conversion to Christ.

Back in 1934, Hamilton was charged with murdering two highway motorcycle patrolmen near Grapevine, Texas. A farmer, testifying he was in his field 50 feet away from the shooting, positively identified Hamilton as one of the killers. While Hamilton was in jail awaiting trial, Bonnie and Clyde were killed. Tests of their guns revealed that they had killed the patrolmen. The farmer admitted that he was not in his field that day. His motive for false witness was the reward money.

Comments Hamilton, "Had the case gone to court before Bonnie and Clyde's guns were seized, I would certainly have been sentenced to the electric chair. I would have been executed, an innocent man. I am against capital punishment because if the court makes a mistake, it cannot give a man his life back. But I believe a convicted first-degree murderer should receive a life sentence." Many, like Hamilton, who falter at capital punishment for fear of committing some irrevocable injustice, hold that by a sentence of life imprisonment a life is symbolically taken.

Despite these objections to capital punishment, the Bible seems to provide for the forfeiture of a murderer's life. However, capital punishment should never be pronounced on anyone without due and full process of law, including capable defense assistance. No one should be executed unless his guilt has been established beyond the slightest doubt, and only then in the absence of mitigating factors. One scholar makes the interesting comment that in Judaism in the centuries just before the coming of Christ, such safeguards were set up to protect the interests of the accused and to make his condemnation so difficult that few were ever put to death. "Such was the Jewish shrinking from the final penalty that there was a saying that a Sanhedrin which put one man to death in seven years might be called 'murderous' " (William Barclay, *The Ten Commandments for Today,* Harper and Row, N.Y.).

Interestingly, New York State recently restored a limited death penalty. Death is now mandatory on conviction for the murder of a policeman or employee of a correctional facility, as well as for a murderer who kills again while serving a life sentence. This raises a question. Is the life of a policeman, even though he risks his life to protect our rights, of greater value than an ordinary citizen? Are not all made in the image of God?

At any rate, an executioner who acts in behalf of constituted authority by releasing the gas in the gas chamber or closing the circuit of the electric chair is not committing murder.

Just War　　War is hell. Someone said, "In war, fathers bury sons instead of sons burying fathers." The pacifist, believing all war is wrong, claims that nonviolence serves peace, justice, and love more effectively than does war. Thus, his duty to heavenly citizenship takes priority over military service.

On the other hand, some who agree that war is wrong hold that in certain situations peace would be a worse wrong. They appeal to both Old and New Testaments for vindication of a "just war." Nothing in the Old Testament suggests it is inconsistent to be at one and the same time a soldier and a follower of the Lord God of hosts. An estimated 30 times God commanded His people to use armed force in carrying out His divine purpose. In the New Testament Paul emphatically declares the divinely established authority of the state to bear the sword (Rom. 13:3). The repentant soldier is never told to quit his profession (Luke 3:14).

Not only is a police force needed within a society, but military force may be required to resist aggressor nations. If unjustly attacked, a country should rightfully defend itself against such lawlessness for the sake of its own people and of justice. To react with nonviolence to an aggressive opponent who lacks any sense of justice usually confirms the aggressor in his inhumanity. Turning the national cheek may be national suicide.

To the argument that violence is destructive comes the reply that some things ought to be destroyed. Do we permit a murderer with a sawed-off shotgun to roam the streets shooting any and all he chooses? Do we let a hijacker terrorize flight crew and passengers if there is a chance to subdue him? Do we let dictators seize helpless nations? Is it wrong to use force on local criminals or international bandits? Someone remarked, "There are no pacifists at the gates of Auschwitz."

The advice of nonresistance to evil in the Sermon on the Mount deals with relationships on an interpersonal basis, not with the larger question of war. Jesus was talking about the believer's reaction to one or two neighbors—the man-to-man ethic, the personal enemy—not the national enemy.

Dietrich Bonhoeffer, the young German pastor who died in prison just before the Allied victory and whose devotional writings have blessed many, inclined toward pacifism in his youth. Yet he became convinced, along with others, that the Hitler regime was so evil and so unstoppable by political and pacifistic methods that the line of Christian duty pointed to resistance against his own nation. Finally he joined in a plot to assassinate Hitler.

Though war may sometimes be the lesser of evils, the Christian must resort to it only when every alternative has been explored and exhausted. He must seek to limit the extent of the conflagration, prevent atrocities, and fight only in self-defense or to protect the weak. Life-taking in this situation is under the responsibility of the state and is not murder.

Summing up, murder (the kind of killing forbidden by the sixth commandment) is the willful, unauthorized taking of human life.

Kinds of Murder Forbidden

Many people have the idea that the commandment against murder is so plain and obvious that it cannot be misunderstood. Often they don't realize that some of the most controversial issues of the past and present hinge on the interpretation of this commandment. We have already touched briefly on some of these—war, capital punishment, self-defense. Other related topics deserve major treatment, but can be discussed here only briefly.

Suicide　The late Warden Lawes tells how one night at Sing-Sing prison a condemned murderer was scheduled for the electric chair. The warden kept the lines open from the governor's mansion in Albany for any possible reprieve, but none came. Just about the time of the execution an old man in a nearby cell tried to hang himself, but was cut down in the nick of time. Ironically, the condemned man wanted to live but died, while the attempted suicide wanted to die but lived. Had he succeeded, he would have been as guilty of murder as the condemned man. Suicide is self-murder.

In this area judgment should be minimal and sympathy maximum, for often a suicide is not in complete control of his mind. In any event, the taking of one's own life is a prerogative which belongs not to us but to God.

Abortion　With half a million cases in a recent year, legal abortion has been called the fastest-growing social revolution in the nation. The main question is—at what point in time does the fetus become human?

Suppose a man hunting deer sees movement in the forest but does not know whether it's another hunter or a deer. Should he shoot without finding out? The answer is obvious. He should withhold fire till he is absolutely certain that it is not human life. Similarly, should not one hesitate to take action against a fetus unless he is absolutely certain it is not human life? Since an embryo is a potential human being, and since we do not know when it becomes human, would it not be wise to exercise charity because of doubt?

Theologian Paul Ramsay of Princeton suggests that, since brain activity is an important consideration in deciding the exact moment of death, electrical activity of the fetal brain should be vital in deciding the beginnings of life. (Fetal brain activity is already readable at eight weeks!)

The National Association of Evangelicals at a recent annual convention passed a resolution which affirmed

> its conviction that abortion on demand for reasons of personal convenience, social adjustment, or economic advantage is morally wrong. At the same time we recognize the necessity for therapeutic abortions to safeguard the health or the life of the mother as in the case of tubular pregnancies. Other pregnancies, such as those resulting from rape or incest, may require deliberate termination, but the decision should be made only after there has been medical, psychological, and religious counseling of the most sensitive kind.

Mercy-killing   A young medical student suffered a great temptation. His father was dying of an incurable disease. The youthful intern thought of giving his father a fatal overdose. His father, sensing his son's thoughts, asked him not to do it. The son resisted the temptation. His father died not long after. Thirty years later the doctor still had the sense of satisfaction that he had never once played God during those years, for, said he, "I never knowingly killed anyone."

Mercy-killing raises many questions. Who makes the decision? Who carries it out? How? Potential abuse opens the way to get rid of the aged and infirm, plus a whole class of unwanted as in Hitler's Germany. The sixth commandment reminds us that the power of life and death belong to God.

Mercy-killing should be distinguished from mercy-dying. If a doctor gives medication to speed death, that's murder. But if a doctor withdraws medication or machine from a terminal patient to permit natural death, this need not be morally wrong. When a person is kept alive only by machine, pulling the plug may be an act of mercy, for it lessens suffering by allowing earlier death. Letting the patient die naturally is not wrong, but taking a life is. God is responsible for the former; man is guilty if he does the latter.

Miscellaneous   Half-killing a person is forbidden. Since each command prohibits the worst possible violation in its particular sphere of morality, the prohibition against murder includes all lesser injury to human life. Knifing, shooting, striking, bombing, and all acts of bodily assault are proscribed. Any deed which tends to injure, maim, or shorten human life is included in this command.

Whatever the degree, all physical violence is wrong, as is the slow torture of mental cruelty, for the intent to harm is forbidden. Failure to observe safety standards by making inflammable toys or clothing, or in driving, may contribute to needless death. This too is wrong.

Withholding food, clothing, or shelter is inhumane. A neighbor's garment given as a pledge was not to be kept overnight, for it was the neighbor's covering (Ex. 22:26-27). Covered in this command are oppression of workers by withholding wages (James 5:4); child labor, as when youngsters not yet in their teens worked in the mines from morning till night, rarely seeing the light of day; exploitation of any kind; exorbitant rents from slum landlords who never repair broken-down, rarely heated tenements; and, of course, slavery, that horrible practice that treats humans like so much merchandise.

A historian tells of a boat sailing from Africa to Jamaica with 400 slaves aboard. When several became ill, the captain feared they might infect others. Using the "jettison clause" in the insurance contract, he drove 132 slaves overboard. This clause promised payment for any part of a cargo which had to be jettisoned to save the rest. When the case was tried, the question was not murder, but whether throwing the slaves overboard was a genuine jettison or a cheat on the insurance company. The verdict ruled the throwing of slaves overboard constituted a legitimate ridding of cargo!

Willful, unnecessary risk of human life as in certain stunts and races is questionable, as is indulgence in harmful habits of gluttony, drinking, smoking, or drug use which damage or lessen life.

Prevention of Murder

Two important principles to help stop murder are: a high regard for life, and the restraint of anger.

Sanctity of life   Hold life in high esteem. The reason a murderer was to be executed was that his victim was made in the image of God (Gen. 9:6). Even after the fall, man bore the image of God, though marred. James contends that we should not curse our fellowman because he is "made after the similitude of God" (3:9). A stab at man is a stab at God. Murder is killing God in effigy.

Sacredness of life was unknown under paganism. The Roman arena with its gladiatorial combats and prisoners thrown to the lions reflected low regard for human beings. But as Christianity gained influence, human beings became more highly regarded.

Stated positively the sixth commandment reads, "Thou shalt honor human life." This command supports the care of health through doctors, nurses, ambulances, hospitals, medicine, first aid, and therapy. (The command was well exemplified by the Good Samaritan.) It also mandates the protection and preservation of life through sanitary measures, non-pollution, cleanliness, safety precautions, good working conditions, and pure food laws.

Suppression of anger   Restrain your temper. Jesus warned that unjustifiable anger was potential murder, as were such harsh expressions as "you empty-head" or "you fool" (Matt. 5:21-22).

In reality, murder begins in the heart with envy, hate, vindictiveness, or prejudice. One, or a combination of these, may lead to slander, false accusation, cursing. The next step would be the actual deed of murder. The sequence is: thought murder, which leads to oral murder, which leads to real murder.

The place to get victory is the beginning stage where murder is still embryonic and hasn't developed into the name-calling stage. But if anger is being rashly verbalized, that's the place to stop before some dastardly deed has ended another's life. "A wrathful man stirreth up strife; but he that is slow to anger appeaseth strife" (Prov. 15:18). Arrest the first emotions of anger. Then anger can never hatch into vindictive speech or vicious act.

Murder Is Forgivable

Three important Bible characters were, in a sense, murderers. Moses slew an Egyptian who was smiting an Israelite. When word got out, Moses had to flee to Midian. King David, after taking Bathsheba, ordered her husband placed in a spot in battle where he would surely be killed. The Apostle Paul confessed that he voted for the death of believers, calling himself a persecutor, injurious, and the chief of sinners (Acts 26:10; 1 Tim. 1:13, 15).

Yet, these three murderers wrote large sections of the Bible. Moses wrote the first five books. David, called a man after God's own heart, wrote many psalms, which have been the devotional literature for both Israel and the church. Paul wrote at least 13 books, about half of the New Testament. Even murder, as heinous a crime as it is, is forgivable through the grace of God, the blood of Christ, and the work of the Spirit.

Yes, there will be murderers in heaven.

8

The Sanctity of Sex

Commandment Seven: "Thou shalt not commit adultery" (Ex. 20:14).

Someone has said, "The time in America is sex o'clock."

TV commercials, billboards, and magazines offer sex as a bonus with everything from toothpaste to cigars. Newspapers are filled with stories of rape, wife-swapping, orgies, perversion, campus cohabitation, homosexuality, and various other forms of sexual immorality. When TV and movies flagrantly flaunt bedroom scenes and marital infidelity, many people are no longer appalled.

Sex in Its Proper Place—a Gift of God

Who invented sex? Some might think *Playboy,* but sex is God-created, God-ordained, and God-blessed. God was the One who implanted physical attraction between the sexes. In itself, sex is not sinful but part of His great plan for mankind. Sex should be accepted with thanksgiving as one of His wonderful gifts.

Dualism, the unbiblical belief which regards the spirit as good but the body as evil, caused many in the medieval church to flee to monasteries, caves, swamps, and deserts to escape fleshly lusts. Marriage was looked upon as something for less spiritual people. Some theologians of the Middle Ages warned married couples that the Holy Spirit left the room when a husband and wife expressed their love physically. Puritanical concepts of sex being sordid and sinful receive no support from Scripture. The Bible plainly states that marriage is honorable, and the bed undefiled (Heb. 13:4).

94

As God's gift, sex is to be expressed in accordance with His design for it. Here's where Christianity differs from the playboy philosophy, which regards sex as only a natural impulse related to nothing ultimate.

What is the divine plan for sex? First, sex expresses the deep oneness of marital love. Second, it propagates the human race. Sex thus relates to both companionship and procreation. Eve was not created primarily for the propagation of the species, but for companionship: God declared it is not good for man to be alone (Gen. 2:18).

Sex is a physical unity which should symbolize a deeper spiritual oneness. The meeting of two bodies cannot of itself express love. Love must exist between two persons before sex can manifest its God-designed purpose. Without love, sex is only a physical thing, animalistic, as in the barnyard. Loveless sex regards a person as a sexual object, debases human beings, and destroys respect for others and self.

A student spending spring vacation on the beach at Fort Lauderdale wore a sweater reading, "Stamp out virginity." A Christian student said to him, "You ought to take that sweater off and put it away in your attic. When you get married and have a little girl and she grows up, the night her first date knocks at the door, go to the attic, get the sweater, and give it to the boy." The first student saw the point. He would want his daughter to be treated like a person, not a thing.

Sex is ordained by God to occur within the context of marriage. To deserve the profound biblical description "one flesh," man and woman must enter a relationship on an enduring basis. The physical aspect is too precious, too personal, too private to be used other than in the context of complete fidelity and permanence of the marriage bond. The physical expression of spiritual love must be preserved for the day when man and woman can give covenant to their devotion publicly. Thereafter, this physical intimacy is to be kept for each other only.

Not only does sex have a unitive function, expressing in a physical way a deep loving oneness, but it gives humans a privilege denied angels—sharing with God in making a new life. Sex normally leads to parenthood, which gives love visible continuity.

But procreation is secondary. Nowhere does the Bible restrict sex to the sole purpose of procreation. On the contrary, the Apostle Paul, by advising against prolonged abstinence from the sex act, implied frequent sexual relations as the norm of marriage—without any mention of procreation (1 Cor. 7:3-5).

If the Bible teaches that sex in marriage is primarily for companionship and secondarily for procreation, it would seem to follow that contraception would be permissible in order to limit the size of one's family.

The Bible encourages married couples to enjoy the gift of sex in its proper context. "Live joyfully with the wife whom thou lovest all the days of thy life" (Ecc. 9:9).

Sex Outside Its Proper Place—Forbidden

Sex should be associated with beautiful words like love, marriage, companionship, home, and babies. Too often it's linked with rape, lust, infidelity, prostitution, and venereal disease. Sex can be a wonderful servant or a terrible master.

Extra-marital affairs   The seventh commandment specifically says, "Thou shalt not commit adultery" (Ex. 20:14). Technically, adultery is illicit sex involving a married person. One sociologist estimated that 60% of husbands and 40% of wives have extra-marital affairs.

A few years ago the *Ladies Home Journal* ran an article titled, "The Affair." It was a condensation of a book which, based on intensive research, concluded that while extramarital affairs may severely damage the participants, their marriages, and innocent bystanders such as children, there are times when such affairs may possibly do good.

That same month the *Reader's Digest* carried an article, "The Case Against Cheating in Marriage." Three arguments against extramarital affairs were presented: they cause pain to the mate; they mask the real problem; they are destructive to the unfaithful partner's self. These damaging effects are known only too well by professional counselors who often have to pick up the pieces.

Jesus did not make light of adultery, nor do the epistles which frequently list it in their catalogs of sins (Gal. 5:19; 1 Cor. 6:9). Many sections in Proverbs warn against involvement with the "strange" or "other" woman (2:16-19; 4:18-20, 23; 6:26-29, 32, 34-35; 7:15, 18-27).

An extramarital affair cannot be anything but unsatisfactory. It lacks public approval. It has no stability. It provides no security for any children born of that union. It is furtive, it is often selfish, at least lacking the quality of total self-giving which finds fulfillment in marriage. It produces a guilt which psychiatry can only make easier to bear but cannot remove, and which is God's warning that His moral law is being violated. Because sex demands a deep and lasting context of a personal commitment for its achievement, extramarital affairs produce frustration and suffering.

Mental adultery   Jesus took the command against adultery from the realm of the overt act to inner thought. "Whosoever looketh on a woman to lust after her hath committed adultery with her already in his heart" (Matt. 5:28). The eye-catching sight of an attractive girl is not wrong, for it is natural to admire beauty. But whoever discovers the impulse to lust through looking and does not turn away but continues to look with lustful intent, is cherishing sinful desire. This is mental adultery.

Obsession with sex   If lustful looks were condemned by Jesus, what judgment would He pronounce on our society for its sick obsession with sex? Commenting on the willingness of an audience to stare at a striptease act, C. S. Lewis imagines a crowd in a theater watching someone display a covered plate. The performer slowly lifts the cover so as to let all see, and just before the lights go out, the plate reveals a mutton chop. Wouldn't we think of such people that something had gone wrong with their appetite for food? Should people gawk wide-eyed at meat every chance they get, even paying to peep, spending time looking at pictures of meat and dribbling saliva and smacking their lips? So, says Lewis, when people gather to watch someone undress on the stage, does it not indicate something wrong with the state of the sex instinct among us? Perhaps women's libbers weren't too far off when they complained that *Playboy* magazine "looks at me like a side of beef."

The emphasis on dirty or suggestive jokes, near nudity, pornography, and filthy literature shows that fallen humanity's imagination is evil continually (Gen. 6:5) and that its eyes are full of adultery that cannot cease from sin (2 Peter 2:14).

Because the Bible deals forthrightly with sex, refusing to gloss over the sexual aberrations of its heroes, the Bible has been called obscene, not fit to be read to mixed audiences. But whether a story is obscene or not depends on how and why it is told. If related to make a jest of sex, to excuse or condone immorality, or to inflame the imagination, it is obscene. But if told to show the sinfulness of sin and its sad consequences, it is not obscene but morally wholesome. The latter is the Bible's purpose. Its plain speaking has rescued many from sex sins and kept others from yielding to temptation.

Also, how different is the Bible from current books which are really obscene! The Bible does not speak of sex with detailed realism, but rather with deep reserve. Any escapade is described in minimum wordage and factual statements. How unlike the juicy paragraphs in filthy books which describe in lavish detail the acts of immoral persons. Librarians tell us that books often fall open at pages containing such extended descriptions, showing that people have read these portions over and over. Though the Bible records immorality with a certain openness, it does so with substantial reserve.

Divorce   Divorce continues on the upswing, according to the Bureau of Census findings. In 1973 there were 63 divorced persons for every 1,000 married persons living with their spouses, compared to 47 in 1970 and 35 in 1960.

In the same section in which He expands adultery to include adulterous thoughts, Jesus also speaks of divorce as related to adultery. "Whosoever shall put away his wife, saving for the cause of fornication, causeth her to commit adultery: and whosoever shall marry her that is divorced committeth adultery" (Matt. 5:32).

Jesus' law of divorce and remarriage is strict when compared to the roughly 30 grounds for divorce in the 50 American states and compared to the laws in much of the rest of world today. Two opposite opinions on divorce were held by the leading schools of thought in Jesus' day. This was known as the Hillel-Shammai dispute. The former taught that a Jew could divorce his wife for almost any reason, whereas the latter held that fornication was the sole lawful grounds. This dispute between the every-cause of Hillel and the one-cause of Shammai, debated all over the land, was not an argument over remarriage but only about the lawful cause of divorce that allowed remarriage (Guy Doty, *Divorce and Remarriage,* Bethany Fellowship, Minneapolis, Minn.).

A choice between these contending viewpoints was what the Pharisees asked of Jesus, "tempting Him." His answer was the same as in the Sermon on the Mount, "Moses because of the hardness of your hearts suffered you to put away your wives, but from the beginning it was not so. And I say unto you, whosoever shall put away his wife, except it be for fornication, and shall marry another, committeth adultery; and whoso marrieth her which is put away doth commit adultery" (Matt. 19:3, 8-9).

Tacitly siding with the stricter school of interpretation, Jesus told the Pharisees that divorce could not be secured on any frivolous grounds. He tossed out every cause except fornication, which in biblical usage refers to sexual immorality whether involving married or unmarried people. Apparently Christ did not abolish all divorce, just the abuse of it, approving divorce and remarriage on the one ground of infidelity.

Some Bible students also add desertion as a scriptural warrant for divorce and remarriage, since desertion is a virtual rupture of the marriage, standing on the same level as adultery (*Pulpit Commentary* on 1 Cor. 7:15).

In our imperfect world, marriage breakups are a fact of life. Divorced people need our compassion. Dr. James M. Boice, pastor of Tenth Presbyterian Church, Philadelphia, comments,

> It is also true that Christians who marry out of God's will and get divorced, remarry (often to Christians) and that God seems often in His great grace to sanctify and bless the remarriage.
>
> Does this mean that in this case God has changed His standards? Not at all. But it does mean that even divorce and remarriage, serious though they are, are not unforgivable and that God is always able to start with His children precisely where they are and bring blessing.

The church should never be closed to such people, and we above all men should show mercy. For perhaps even if such persons marry in rebellion against God's will He may bring repentance. And He may yet greatly bless the new home ("The Biblical View of Divorce," *Eternity,* December 1970).

Playboy philosophy   The seventh commandment rules out adultery in its technical sense, adulterous thoughts, and adulterous divorce. Beyond that, it prohibits every type of sin which invades the sanctum of sex. It runs directly counter to today's playboy philosophy.

This modern hedonism says, in effect, that erotic love is the real meaning of life and brings unending happiness. Choosing a wife is mainly selecting a good sex partner. If sex attraction fades, divorce or affairs are permissible. Teenagers should be given full information and access to contraceptives. Pregnancy can be solved by abortion. This attitude deifies sex, making it an end in itself, an idol to be worshiped. (Sexual promiscuity and idolatry have long been associated. Heathen temples employed prostitute-priestesses. The temple at Corinth had 1,000 at the time of Paul.) Today multitudes bow at the shrine of sex.

The playboy attitude perverts true love which is other-person centered. It overrides qualities such as loyalty, responsibility, and consideration. It downgrades personality by treating persons as mere things to be used for one's gratification.

Premarital sex   A much-advertised attitude today goes like this: if two people are in love and have a meaningful relationship, premarital sex is permissible. This view is sometimes called the new morality.

Such a relationship cannot be God-pleasing since His plan restricts sex to marriage. God's Word calls sex outside marriage *fornication,* one of the sins Jesus condemned (Mark 7:21). Biblical condemnation of premarital sex should be sufficient for anyone who wants to live under the sway of God's Word. To call chastity before marriage "hogwash" is to say, "God, You don't know what You're talking about." Wouldn't the all-wise God, who created sex, know whether premarital sex is right or wrong?

Good reason exists apart from biblical prohibition for regarding unchastity as wrong. Premarital sex, rather than being meaningful and of mutual benefit, can on the contrary ultimately bring hurt to both parties. The relationship can be robbed of its fullest potential by a cheap and shallow substitution.

Two young people say, "We're going to get married. We are deeply in love, and are so certain to marry we don't want to wait to have sex. Why should we wait?"

Their marrying isn't certain. One midwestern Christian college faculty member estimated that each year 25% of engaged couples on that campus broke their engagements. No couple thinks they'll be the ones who won't get married, but it happens over and over. Several couples who swore they were in love broke their engagements just a few days before the wedding dates. That's why the seal of marriage is so important. It provides the turning point that forces a couple to be sure this is a life commitment.

People have an amazing capacity to rationalize that theirs is a meaningful relationship. A few visits to each other's apartment or a few minutes in the back seat of a car convinces them they are in love. Such liaisons break up all the time. Thus, couples should wait till marriage before engaging in sexual intercourse.

Those who advocate trial marriage forget that one of the ingredients of real marriage is commitment. If commitment is missing, it's not a real marriage they're trying.

Here are some comments by young people who believe it best to wait till marriage:

- "Sex involves total people. That's why 10 minutes in the back seat of a car ruins the beauty of sex."
- "Sex before marriage is a sort of playing at house, a poor substitute for the real thing."
- "Having sex with someone else, no matter how much you think you're in love, eats away at your trust in each other. You know the other as an experimenter. Sex can ruin a beautiful friendship."
- "Some couples see no point in a ceremony that proclaims you married. But I think a ceremony says you're committing yourself to something serious from which you don't just walk away. If love isn't enough to seal publicly, it's not real enough to express sexually."

Homosexuality   The gays have now come out of the closets into the streets. On TV talk shows, homosexuals discuss their lifestyle without shame or inhibition. A council of 50 Protestant ministers in the San Francisco area recently organized with the express aim of getting churches to drop their condemnation of homosexuals and to welcome them into full fellowship.

Let's make a few observations. First, homosexuality is not a normal way of life. It has been called a pathetic little second-rate substitute for reality, a misuse of the sexual faculty of human construction. God's plan does not involve two men or two women but one male and one female.

Second, we must always distinguish between a person with homosexual tendencies and a practicing homosexual. The former could find acceptance and strength within the church to keep his propensities from developing into acts. But homosexual deeds must ever be judged wrong in the light of the Bible.

Third, virtually all societies in history have condemned homosexuality. Not long ago in the Arab country of Yemen, a 60-year-old man convicted of this vice was executed by shooting in a city square before a crowd of 6,000. *Time* magazine, reporting this incident, stated that the only society apart from some primitive ones that distinctly approved of homosexual love was 5th-century B.C. Greece.

Fourth, God's judgment on homosexuality is revealed in the opening book of the Bible. Because Sodom was given over to this practice, God destroyed it (Gen. 19). The New Testament also condemns it (Rom. 1:26-27). Let's not think our society immune from God's judgment if we condone this perversion.

Two homosexuals recently engaged in a "marriage" ceremony in a Washington, D.C., church that caters to homosexuals. They said they wanted God to bless their union. But how can the church or anyone else change the law of God to accommodate man's sinful desires? Though the sinner should be treated with fairness and understanding, the vice merits no encouragement, glamorization, or rationalization.

God's Word includes practicing homosexuals among those who shall not inherit the kingdom of God (1 Cor. 6:9). Compassion for the homosexual includes telling him the truth of God's revelation, pointing out the ultimate penalty of persistent violation of

God's command, and holding out the promise of forgiveness where there is repentance, which always involves turning away from sinful conduct.

Venereal disease   One evidence of divine displeasure on sexual immorality is venereal disease, which now is no laughing matter. The chief doctor at the Venereal Disease Clinic at Bellevue Center, New York University Medical School, estimates a round figure of 5 million cases of gonorrhea in the U.S.—roughly one out of 40 citizens. Since the vast majority of venereal disease is found in the 15-29 age bracket, reputable authorities state it not inconceivable that over half the people in that age-group are infected (*Journal News,* Nyack, N.Y., Dec. 30, 1970). We cannot play fast and loose with God's laws and get away with it.

Sex—Help to Keep It in Proper Place

In forbidding mental adultery, Jesus gave this advice "If thy right eye offend thee, pluck it out . . . If thy right hand offend thee, cut it off" (Matt. 5:29-30). Remove from your life anything that causes you to sin. Deliberate exposure to filth in today's literature or on the movie or TV screen can easily lead to mental adultery, and certainly fails to contribute to a healthy thought life. Do not intentionally position yourself in the place of temptation. A proverb says, "He who would not enter the room of sin must not sit at the door of temptation."

Watch your thinking. Get victory in the early stage—the thought stage. You may not be able to keep an evil thought from flitting into your mind. The trouble comes when we dwell on a thought, encouraging it to grow into a fascinating image. David's sin was entertaining a lustful thought about Bathsheba till it snowballed into adultery, and then into murder. Remember the good example of Joseph, who, propositioned by Potiphar's wife, fled her allurements. Paul wrote, "Flee also youthful lusts" (2 Tim. 2:22).

Fill your mind with good thoughts. "Whatsoever things are pure . . . lovely . . . think on these things" (Phil. 4:8). One Christian youth told his pastor that his personal purity and thought life were directly related to his spending time with the Lord day by day. The patriarch Job wrote, "I made a covenant with mine eyes; why then should I think upon a maid?" (Job 31:1)

If you've broken the seventh commandment and are sorry, take heart from the dealings of the Saviour with the woman of Samaria who had had five husbands and who was living with a man not her husband (John 4:18). After encountering Christ, she was not only cleansed but became a fruitful winner of souls. Also take heart from the words of Jesus to the woman taken in the very act of adultery, "Neither do I condemn thee; go, and sin no more" (John 8:11).

9

Is Honesty the Guest Policy?

Commandment Eight: "Thou shalt not steal" (Ex. 20:15).

A woman shopping in a high-class department store in northern New Jersey asked to try on a fairly expensive coat. She was surprised when the clerk had to unlock the chain around that rack of coats. Later, in another fine store, as she walked into an alcove of fairly high-priced dresses, a bell sounded. The clerk explained that any person crossing into that area broke a beam of light which activated a bell to alert store personnel that someone was there. "We do this," she added, "because so much merchandise has been stolen from under our noses."

Shoplifting has reached mammoth proportions in our country. A woman, seemingly pregnant, walked out of a store to "give birth" to a pound of butter, a chuck roast, a bottle of pancake syrup, and packages of toothpaste, candy, and hair tonic. One California mother was observed tapping various articles as she made her way through a supermarket, followed by her two children who pocketed the designated items. One estimate said that one out of every 52 supermarket customers carries away at least one item not paid for. The other 51 will pay more for their food to compensate for the estimated $3 billion annual loss.

Not all the stealing is done by the customers. A man counted the number of tablets in a 100-vitamin bottle to discover only 90 in it. Investigators found boxes advertising 100 screws with only 60 inside. Over 500 randomly selected products—office supplies, housewares, medicine, foodstuffs—were counted and found to be deficient of quantity promised in nearly half the cases. One package of "eight" frozen lobster tails had only six. A Bureau of Weights and Measures official estimates that total loss to U.S. consumers from short counting is nearly $3 million a year.

Against cheating by store or shopper, and against dishonesty in every area of life, thunders the eighth commandment: "Thou shalt not steal!"

What This Command Assumes—Private Ownership

Stealing is taking that which is not rightfully yours. Unless things can be owned by people, stealing has no meaning. This commandment tacitly recognizes the right of private ownership of property.

In Marxist philosophy, which holds that the "Haves" are the oppressors of the "Have-nots," the eighth commandment is regarded as the source of evil. "Thou shalt not steal" is considered an economic stratagem to continue the prosperity of the ruling class and the oppression of the masses. Since the wealthy and the poor are enemies, the proletariat is urged to liquidate the bourgeoisie by revolution, confiscate their wealth, and create a classless society in which the prevailing dictum will be "from each according to his ability, to each according to his need." For the "Have-nots," who compose most of the world's population, Communist ideology which does away with private ownership of property has tremendous appeal.

When the pooling of property and goods in the Early Church is cited as an example of Christian Communism, a striking difference should be kept in mind. The Early Church shared voluntarily; Marxism takes forcibly. Christianity says, "What is mine is yours." Communism says, "What is yours is mine."

Even voluntary collective ownership never seems to have worked well throughout history. William Bradford, governor of Plymouth Colony during its formative years, tells how the initial policy of cultivating the lands in common, and of sharing the produce collectively, was replaced by private ownership (*Of Plymouth Plantation,* 1620-47). When property was owned by the community, strong young men complained about working for other men's wives and children without pay. Men who worked harder thought it unjust that men who didn't work with the same zeal should receive the same amount of food and clothing. Wives who had to do service for other men, like preparing their meat or washing their clothes, considered it slavery, nor did their husbands like it.

But when the governor assigned to every man a parcel of land according to the size of his family, and gave to each family its own corn, everyone became industrious. Much more corn was planted. Work was done willingly, harvest brought plenty, and the more industrious had a surplus to sell, so that want and famine disappeared.

What This Command Forbids—Stealing

Obviously bank robberies, street hold-ups, and house burglaries are forbidden, but stealing can be done in many different ways. Thievery is almost a way of life for many with the philosophy "You only go round once, so be sure to grab your share of the action." Deeply entrenched in the American system is a web of graft, bribery, pay-offs, extortion, confidence rackets, and octopus crime syndicates.

Some who would never overtly or forcibly take another's property find it easy to rob impersonal organizations "who would never miss the little we take." The manager of an aircraft company ordered workers to assemble in the yard for a group photograph, but the guilt-ridden workers thought it to be an inspection. Suddenly the ground was littered with quickly abandoned tools and equipment they had hidden away in their lockers.

One motel owner commented, "We're all thieves at heart. Show me a person who says he's never pinched anything from a motel or hotel and I'll show you a liar." When one hearer affirmed innocence, the owner jeered, "Not even a towel?"

The hearer admitted defeat, for he had been a towel-snitcher a few times. "They fit perfectly into my little zipper bag," he protested in defense.

The owner continued, "Towels aren't very much. Sheets are what most people pinch. And some steal anything that's not nailed down, even coffee dispensers and TV sets."

One hotel manager, realizing that ball-point pens were being stolen from room desks, put up a sign: "Pens like this may be purchased from the room clerk for the sum of 35 cents." The following week twice as many pens were stolen!

A girl with a recent M.A. in retailing, on her first job one week, spied a lovely dress which she couldn't afford. Her supervisor, noting how badly the new clerk wanted it, ripped off a button from the coveted dress, exclaiming, "Now that the dress is damaged, we'll have to mark it down!" The girl got the dress for half price, and, added someone, "A Ph.D. in cheating."

When employers fail to give a full day's wage for a full day's work, that's dishonest. When an employee fails to give a full day's work for a full day's pay, that's stealing, as is shoddy or deceptive work. When a repairman replaced the motor on a dishwasher, the woman insisted on keeping the old motor which she had a mechanic-friend check out. The only thing wrong was grease on the electrical contact, so she stopped payment on the $45 check given the repairman. She then wrote the appliance service company asking for a reduction in the service call charge. She never got an answer.

Insurance companies are bilked out of thousands of dollars in false claims. Take the case of a successful businessman, president of a large corporation at a salary of $40,000 plus a year. One day, crossing Broadway in New York City, he dropped his gold fountain pen for which he had paid $75 years before. A bus smashed it to pieces. Since his personal loss and theft policy did not cover that type of accident, he put in a claim, telling the insurance agent that he had lost his pen. The agent, never questioning his honesty, advised the company to pay. A few days after receiving a check for $75, the corporation president boasted to his friends of the virtues of insurance.

One well-dressed woman, in a fine restaurant where the feature was a dessert table to which you could return as many times as you wished, made repeated trips to the table of delicacies. On returning to her seat, when she thought no one was watching, she deposited the desserts in a large shopping bag by her feet.

Newsweek magazine told of a lavish country club overseas frequented by high-ranking U.S. military officers. Players' golf games are aided by trained caddies who are able, while walking along, to grab a golf ball between the big toe and second toe without breaking stride, and to deposit it in perfect position for the next shot.

Academic cheating is widespread. Students search thick fraternity house files to find essays they can copy, or hire ghostwriters to do the job. One New York group of recent college graduates turns out term papers ranging from a short theme on existentialism to a full thesis on Chilean politics at fees ranging from $60 to $500. Some students get advance copies of exams by breaking into offices, or bribing secretaries. Others pay a student to take the exam for them.

Carelessness with other people's property is a form of stealing. County workmen in New Jersey made an unexpected catch in the local brook. Clearing debris from the stream, they fished out about 200 shopping carts, each costing the supermarket at least $35. Most of the carts were broken or twisted, apparently dumped into the stream from the parking lots behind the stores by patrons after loading groceries into their cars. Thefts of such carts may total as much as $15 million yearly.

One Sunday morning, in the middle of the 19th century, in the old Oberlin meetinghouse, revivalist Charles Finney used for a sermon subpoint, "The Sin of Borrowing Things and Not Returning Them." His comment was pointed. "When I went to my toolhouse yesterday with some men on hand to do my work, I found it practically empty. President Mahan had borrowed my plow and never sent it back. Professor Morgan had sent for my spade, and I don't know where it is. Deacon Beecher has had one of my monkey wrenches for so long a time that the memory of man cannot recall how long ago it was borrowed. What does it mean," he shouted eloquently, "that among the best of us there is such a carelessness concerning our fundamental everyday obligations?"

The sermon was most effective, for next morning before dawn one conscience-stricken neighbor tried to restore a sawhorse which belonged to Finney and he had to be rescued from Finney's watchdog. All the rest of the morning there was a stream of neighbors' boys carrying borrowed tools—only a part of which Finney could recognize as his property!

Modern business is known to possess its share of questionable and even dishonest practices. Someone said, "A man can steal from a railroad car and go to jail for months, but if a man can steal the whole railroad, that's business acumen."

We have dealt with stealing from our fellowmen, not with stealing from God, which is possible, for the Prophet Malachi asked, "Will a man rob God?" When asked, "How do men rob God?" the prophet replied, "In tithes and offerings" (Mal. 3:8). By withholding the tenth of their income, or by failing to use the resources which God loans them, God's people are guilty of robbing Him.

What the Command Requires—Stewardship

Stewardship is the antithesis of stealing. The wider implications of the eighth commandment are discussed in Paul's letter to the Ephesians, "Let him that stole steal no more, but rather let him labor, working with his hands the thing which is good, that he may have to give to him that needeth" (4:28).

1. Honesty "Steal no more." A young man tells how one day a stranger came to his door and offered to buy his father's car. The family was poor and in need of money. The boy thought of what the extra cash could buy, for the man offered a high price. But to his amazement he heard his father explain that the car had something seriously wrong with it, and was not worth that much. To put it in good shape would cost several hundred dollars.

The stranger who thought the car looked good and couldn't see this defect naturally did not buy. The boy was disappointed. Later, however, he began to appreciate his father's honesty which meant continued financial depression rather than several hundred dollars—with a guilty conscience. His father's selfless act helped him to the path of honesty.

2. Work "Let him labor." There is nothing wrong or un-dignified with good, hard, honest work. When a famous author was carrying in his winter's supply of coal, a neighbor told him that it was undignified for a man of his reputation to perform such menial work. The author replied, "The man who is ashamed to carry his own coal deserves to sit all winter by an empty fireplace!"

The gospel accounts are full of busy, hurrying people: fishing, farming, traveling, cleaning rooms, digging. Not an idler seemingly appears, except the man who hid his talent and was rebuked. "Go work in my vineyard" was the command to those in need of employment (see Matt. 20:6-7).

In fact, God works. The Lord Jesus was a carpenter. Before the fall God ordered man to work, dressing and keeping the garden (Gen. 2:15). To the Thessalonians Paul wrote, "If any would not work, neither should he eat" (2 Thes. 3:10).

It almost goes without saying that our occupation should be an honorable, not a questionable one. Paul said, "Working . . . the thing which is good."

3. *Industry*   The phrase "working with his hands" seems to imply hard work. Someone has said, "The ladder of success cannot be climbed with your hands in your pockets." Many proverbs inveigh against sloth and exhort to diligence (see 6:6-11). Someone else said, "Our forefathers thought nothing of working 16 hours a day, and neither does this generation."

A Christian should work industriously, whether on his own or under the eye of a supervisor. Ever hear of the man in a boat in the middle of the lake when a terrific storm came up and dumped him overboard? With powerful strokes he swam toward shore, leaving no doubt as to his ability to make it. But just 50 feet from safety, the 5 o'clock whistle blew and he stopped swimming and drowned.

Too many employees approach their job with the philosophy, "How little can I do, and how much can I make?" The New Testament says Christians should do their jobs as though working for the Lord (Col. 3:22-24). If we thought of ourselves as employees of Christ, doing our tasks under His watchful eye, how well would we do our work! How faithful would we be in the little things?

A servant girl asked to join a church. When asked how she knew she was converted, she replied, "Because now I sweep under the rugs. I used to be careless when I did the sweeping!" Christ's love so filled her heart that she expressed it the best way she knew. Not a golden-voiced singer who held vast audiences spellbound, nor a famous artist who painted magnificent pictures, but a faithful maid who swept under as well around the rugs. Diligence on the job is a witness to our Lord.

4. Liberality "Give to him that needeth." A major by-product of industrious labor is that not only do we support ourselves and our families, but we have funds left over to give to the needy. Some are unable to work because of illness or accident. These weak individuals are to be supported by the strong, according to the New Testament ethic which teaches that it is more blessed to give than to receive. Christian workers, organizations, missionaries, the poor will need help. Earning much while giving away little is one way of robbing others and God. A service station owner, his face smeared with grime, looked up from the grease pit and said, "I'm earning money to help send missionaries across the ocean, support my church, and aid the poor."

Incidentally, Paul's statement to the Ephesians contains the three ways of acquiring possessions. The first is the wrong method; the second and third are legitimate ways (4:28).

(1) Wrong—Stealing—"Let him that stole"
(2) Right—Working—"let him labor"
(3) Right—Receiving as a gift—"that he may have to give to him that needeth"

The two rights ways of obtaining property are labor and liberality. It has been suggested that gambling is wrong (apart from other considerations) because whatever is won does not come through either one's work or another's generosity. The winner has not labored for it. Nor has the loser donated it to the winner in the spirit of charity. Rather, the loser has gambled in the hope of taking something away from his opponent, not losing it. If love prevailed, there would be giving, not gambling.

Forgiveness for Stealing

Stealing is a sin which needs divine forgiveness through the shed blood of Jesus Christ. It was a sin of the traitor Judas, whom the New Testament specifically calls a thief (John 12:6).

During His ministry the Lord called many tax collectors, who because of their job were likely guilty of lining their pockets through dishonest overcharges. Significantly, Zaccheus, the rich chief tax collector of Jericho, on his conversion stated he would make restitution, paying back fourfold to those whom he had defrauded (Luke 19:8). Equally interesting was his vow to give half his goods to the poor. Stewardship is the opposite of stealing.

All who have cheated fellowmen and would have a conscience void of offense toward God and toward man, like Zaccheus, should both receive Christ into their hearts and then make amends to the persons they have cheated.

Since 1811, when someone who had defrauded the government anonymously sent $5 to Washington, the U.S. Treasury has operated a Conscience Fund. In 1974 money sent in totaled over $44,000, making the grand total since the beginning over $3.3 million. One 1974 note written in a shaky hand in black ink on lined looseleaf paper stated that the writer was sending $10 for blankets taken in World War II. "My mind could not rest. Sorry I am so late." It was signed by an ex-GI.

Another man sent $50 to cover the cost of two pairs of cavalry boots, two pairs of trousers, a case of K rations, and 30 pounds of fresh meat he had stolen from the Army between 1943 and 1946. Restitution makes it right with man. But to make it right with God requires repentance.

Once a week a factory owner invited a preacher to address his workers in their dining hall during an extended lunch hour. In a question-and-answer period after a noon-day sermon, one worker stood and said bluntly, "We don't need religion. We have everything we want. Our wages are good. The firm provides recreation. Food is served at noon. We don't even have to clear away or wash the dishes. What need do we have of religion?"

The preacher asked the audience to turn and look at a poster on the back wall, remarking, "There's my answer." The poster read: "1,200 knives and forks have been stolen from this dining hall during the past month. In the future, those using this dining hall must bring their own cutlery." Commented the preacher "Men, you do need something. You need a Person, the Lord Jesus Christ, who died for our sins and who has the power to help us live honestly. The first convert of the Saviour on the cross was the dying thief who repented. And if you'll repent, He'll forgive you. And you'll return any knives or forks you have taken."

10

To Tell the Truth

Commandment Nine: "Thou shalt not bear false witness" (Ex. 20:16).

A small boy approached a stranger, "Mister, have you lost a dollar?"

The stranger replied, "Yes, I believe I have. Did you find it?"

Exclaimed the little lad, "Oh, no. I just wanted to find out how many people have lost a dollar today, and you make the 55th person!"

Over 200 New Yorkers were handed a doctored list of magazines, some current, a few deceased, and a couple of phonies. They were asked to point out the ones they read regularly. Nine percent said they read *Collier's*. Asked which magazine they would keep if they could have but one, seven percent chose *Collier's*. The last issue of *Collier's* was published in 1957!

Human depravity is widely displayed through lying. "The wicked . . . go astray as soon as they [are] born, speaking lies," says the psalmist (Ps. 58:3). Even a baby may lie by crying in pretended hunger or hurt when in reality he wants attention. A child, told not to touch the jam, takes some, then when asked if he has taken any says no with the telltale evidence all over his mouth.

Despite its prevalency, lying is a sin God forbids. "Lying lips are abomination to the Lord" (Prov. 12:22). Though many regard lying as harmless slips of speech, among seven things God hates two refer to lying (Prov. 6:16-19), "a lying tongue" and "a false witness." Paul says, "Lie not one to another, seeing that ye have put off the old man with his deeds" (Col. 3:9). The ninth commandment reads, "Thou shalt not bear false witness."

What Is a Lie?

A simple definition of lying would be: saying that which is not true with intent to deceive.

Kidding is not lying. One April 1st a lady received a phone call from her sister to go into the kitchen to look for an article supposedly left there. After a brief search failed to locate the object, the lady returned to the phone to hear, "April Fool." The sister would be considered jesting, not lying.

A mistake in a statement is not a lie. When a broadcaster announces that 20 people were killed in a plane crash, and the number turns out to be 19, he may be reporting erroneous information, but he is not lying, for there is no intent to deceive.

A work of fiction is not a lie. Some years ago a Christian leader suggested that Christians should not read fiction, because the fictitious bordered on prevarication. Yet Jesus spoke many parables, which though true to life were non-factual or make-believe. But they were given to illustrate truth, not to deceive people.

The use of figurative language is not lying. When Jesus called Himself the door, this was not literal truth, for He is not wood, hinges, and knob. He used that metaphor to teach that He is the entrance to heaven. Neither is hyperbole deceit, such as the statement about the many other things Jesus did, which if recorded "even the world itself could not contain the books that should be written" (John 21:25). Of course, figurative language should never be employed to create a false impression.

Polite formalities should not be classified as lies. When an acquaintance asks how you are, and you reply, "Fine, thank you," though you have a stomachache, your answer should not be considered a lie, for passing neighbors are not really interested in the state of your health. That reply is just part of a cultural ritual.

Deceit, where the rules of the game call for it, is not lying. When Allied invasion forces landed in Normandy on D-Day, the German Luftwaffe was on a wild goose chase over France, sent there because of Allied interference with German radar. Deceit is an expected strategy of war, as well as of sports. A football quarterback does his best to fool his opponents as to what he will do with the ball.

Action contrary to one's previous statement is not lying, when unforeseen circumstances lead him to alter his previous intent. Though Peter at first said to Christ, "Thou shalt never wash my feet," a few words from Christ caused Peter to beg Him to wash not only his feet, but his hands and heads as well (John 13:6-9). However, deviation from one's previous word is not permissible if such a change would circumvent an obligation to God or man. A professor who months in advance signs a contract to teach at a certain college, and then a week before school opens receives an offer to teach at another college (at a much better salary), breaks his word if he violates the first contract.

It is no lie to conceal or withhold part of the truth when it is not expedient or necessary to tell it. When Samuel was commanded by the Lord to anoint a son of Jesse king, he said, "How can I go? If Saul hears it, he will kill me." And the Lord said, "Take an heifer with thee, and say, 'I am come to sacrifice to the Lord'" (1 Sam. 16:2). Saul had no right to know the entire purpose of Samuel's mission to Jesse, nor was Samuel under obligation to reveal it. Concealment by Samuel was not lying.

How intolerable life would be if we were required to disclose all truth. Withholding truth is often both necessary and kind. "A talebearer revealeth secrets; but he that is of a faithful spirit concealeth the matter" (Prov. 11:13).

Probably the most knotty problem relating to lying has to do with telling a lie to do good, such as saving someone's life. The Gestapo agent has come to search a house in which a Jewish wife is hiding, and at the door asks the husband if anyone is inside. Should he tell the soldier the truth and get her killed, or should he lie to save her life? This ethical area is sometimes called the "tragic moral choice." The two major schools of thought on this problem are known as the "greater good" and "lesser evil" theories.

When Rahab lied about the whereabouts of the spies to save their lives, according to the "greater good" school of thought she was doing right, for saving a life is more important than telling the truth. The saving of a life not only annuls the lower law against lying, but makes the telling of the lie a good. In fact, according to this view, to tell the truth would be morally wrong, for it would be abetting murder.

Those who hold the other view, though commending Rahab for her action in saving the spies, insist that the New Testament commends her solely for her faith in receiving the spies and sending them out another way, and does not express approval for her lie. According to this "lesser of two evils" theory, Rahab is commended not because of her lying, but in spite of it. Calvin terms Rahab's act not devoid of the praise of virtue, but not spotlessly pure. On this view a lie is never justifiable. However, both theories agree that when the alternatives of saving a life or lying confront us, the loving choice is to save the life. If lying in this case is evil, God will grant forgiveness. As Peter says, "Charity shall cover the multitude of sins" (1 Peter 4:8).

Ways of Lying

The book *Do You Lie with Finesse?* carried this sub-caption: "The Complete Alibi Handbook will teach you to be a perfect liar and will give you an 'out' for almost every situation." What a variety of ways to lie!

Direct lie   When blind Isaac asked Jacob, "Who art thou, my son?" Jacob answered, "I am Esau thy firstborn" (Gen. 27:18-19). No answer could have been more directly calculated to deceive. Not long ago the director of a well-known parapsychology research center admitted falsifying his experimental data. This was direct deception.

Perjury   A formal lie—a false statement under oath in court—constitutes perjury. Great pains were taken in Old Testament times to see that testimony was reliable and true. Two witnesses were necessary, especially in murder cases. A false witness was not to go unpunished, but instead was to receive the penalty for the crime for which he gave false witness (Deut. 19:16-19).

Half-truth   A little girl whose sister was sick told the teacher that her sister didn't feel like coming to school. The wording was true but left a wrong impression. Someone has said, "Little white lies soon become double features in technicolor."

Quoting out of context A speaker said, "I like Canada better than the U.S. with respect to Sunday observance." He was quoted as saying, "I like Canada better than the U.S.," giving an entirely different meaning. Caution should be exercised by people in Christian circles to quote correctly the remarks of others, especially of those with whom they disagree.

Acted lie A study of a thousand advertising executives who carried brief cases home at night revealed that two-thirds never opened them. They took their brief cases home to impress their bosses.

Lies may be made by a deceptive shrug of the shoulders, emphasis on a portion of a sentence, tone of voice, or by a glance toward the wrong road when asked directions. Joseph's brothers showed their father Joseph's coat of many colors daubed with blood to suggest the lad had been killed by a wild animal, when they knew all along that they had sold him into slavery. Judas planted a kiss of deceit on Jesus in betrayal.

An English detective recently received a three-year prison term after he confessed to planting drugs and other evidence on four men to help gain a promotion in 1969. All four had been convicted as a result of this acted lie, but because of the detective's admission of guilt they were granted pardons and their names were cleared. The detective turned himself in shortly after becoming an elder in a church.

Keeping quiet If I hear a person being defamed on a matter on which I have some facts to the contrary, it is silent participation in the lie to fail to speak out the evidence that would clear the victim's sullied character.

Keeping quiet may take other forms. Many a man has been ruined by untold wealth—wealth not reported on his income tax returns.

Slander, detraction Slander is wrongly imputing vice to another person, whereas detraction is groundless diminishing of another's virtue. Potiphar's wife slandered Joseph when she falsely accused him of attempted rape. When someone remarks, "He's a man with real ability to climb the corporation ladder so quickly," and another replies, "Yes, but he sure knows how to butter up the boss," that's detraction.

Self-detraction   Mock humility about one's abilities or achievements is sometimes uttered to secure a contradiction which feeds the vanity. A highschooler says, "I'm a poor student," when his grades are A's or B's. He makes the understatement because he wants to hear someone say, "You're a smart student. You get good grades."

Boasting   After crossing a bridge an ant on an elephant's back remarked, "My, didn't we shake that bridge!" Overstatement with regard to self is boasting, whether about one's feats, position, salary, grades, or abilities. Or one may magnify his former wicked deeds, making others think him a worse character than he actually was.

Flattery   Someone said, "A flatterer is one who says things to your face that he wouldn't say behind your back." Someone else remarked, "Ninety-four percent of soft soap is lye." Says the psalmist, "With flattering lips and with a double heart do they speak. The Lord shall cut off all flattering lips" (Ps. 12:2-3).

Exaggeration   Pupils were asked to construct a sentence using the word *amphibious.* A fisherman's boy suggested the following: "Most fish stories am fibious." Exaggeration is a form of prevarication. It's possible to exaggerate the attendance at a church service, the number of conversions from a crusade, and the ability of a choir.

Pragmatic lies   Pragmatism, a philosophy of temporal expediency, says that whatever works is right. A lie isn't wrong, except when you're caught, according to this view. A young man in America wrote his missionary parents in Africa that he attended church faithfully every Sunday. The truth was that he rarely went to church, but he knew his lie would make them happy.

After a sermon on "Archaeology and the Bible," a skeptic told a skeptic friend the talk was very unconvincing, but later that evening, meeting a Bible-believing friend, told him that the sermon almost made a believer out of him. The Bible speaks against double-tonguedness, telling one thing to one person, and a different thing to another.

At half-time with his team losing, Knute Rockne, famous Notre

Dame football coach who always had a bag of tricks up his sleeve to win his games, choked up his players when he read them a telegram from his six-year-old son, "I want daddy's team to win."

Rockne commented, "Boys, that youngster of mine is lying in a hospital right now in South Bend. He's a mighty sick lad, and I promised to bring him the football as a present. Are you men going to let the kid down?" Though they took a terrific pounding, they won the game, all for the sick lad. As they walked wearily off the field, who should meet them but a perfectly healthy six-year-old, waving a Notre Dame banner and yelling, "Hooray! My pop's team won!"

Business   A garage announced a special on testing brakes. A neighboring businessman observed, "Unless you watch, they won't even look at the brakes." A company, asked to do a repair job, promised zealously to send a man the next day, knowing full well they couldn't send anyone for at least two weeks because of prior commitments.

A used-car salesman waited on a customer who had picked out a certain car which the salesman knew was in poor condition. The customer asked to be driven home in that car. The salesman marveled that the car performed so well. At his home the customer pulled out his pen and started to sign the purchase papers, then halted, "One question, sir. If you were me, would you buy this car?"

The salesman's heart did a flip-flop. He was broke and needed the commission. While inwardly debating, he looked up and there on the customer's living-room wall was a motto, "God hears every word you say." There was no sale.

Advertising   A recent book subtitled *The Inside Truth About Advertising* gives many examples of tricks of the trade for misleading headlines and distorted TV commercials. For example, one leading meat packer advertised, "One pound of our franks is as nourishing as one pound of steak." But asks the author, "Did you ever try eating ten frankfurters in a pound package—as one meal?" Ads for a hair conditioner stated, "Actually makes your hair feel stronger." A dermatologist commented, "This is advertising nonsense. Scientifically it's baseless."

Some years ago the *Detroit News* carried an ad on page 23 in which baseball's home-run star of that decade, Hank Greenberg, said, "You can't beat Raleighs for less nicotine . . . less throat irritants . . . all round safer smoking. I recommend Raleighs to all my friends." In an interview on page 17 of the same issue Hank Greenberg said, "The doctors said I had a stomach disorder and I'm giving up cigarettes and coffee. I never was much of a smoker anyway. I'm sleeping better now and I feel much better."

Lies to God   "Why hath Satan filled thine heart to lie to the Holy Ghost?" Ananias was asked (Acts 5:3). Unkept vows to God are lies. People vow to attend church regularly, serve faithfully, attend prayer meetings, but fail to keep their word to God. We should follow the example of Hannah who kept her vow to give back to God any child He might loan her (1 Sam. 1:11).

The Mischief of Lying

Lying affects us   A clerk weighed the only chicken left in an ice-packed barrel, and announced, "Five pounds." When the customer said he wanted a bigger one, the clerk put the chicken back in the barrel, then pulled the same chicken out. Putting it on the scales and adding pressure the clerk announced, "Seven pounds."

"That's fine," replied the customer, "I think I'll take both of them."

Lying eventually catches up with us, as in the case of the girl who took 10 days off work, pretending to have the flu. Then she really caught the bug and had to work while actually ill in order to cover up the lie. "It was awful," she moaned.

Lying affects the liar. Since we were meant to possess truth in the inward parts, lying lowers self-respect. In addition, if we persist, our credibility will be doubled. Also, one lie leads to another till we become hopelessly tangled in the octopus of deceit. Mark Twain put it, "If you tell the truth, you don't have to remember anything."

Lying affects others   Lying disrupts the fabric of society which operates on a supposed foundation of truth. If a person turned on his TV to watch a 9 P.M. program, only to find the program had just ended, what havoc a continued practice of this would create, especially if deliberately done by the *TV Guide.* Or, if you arrived at the airport for the 7 P.M. jet to Los Angeles to discover it wouldn't leave till midnight, a steady diet of such timetable deceptions would soon confuse the public into a hopeless lack of confidence.

Lying leads others to think truth unimportant. If parents lie, should they complain if their children likewise practice duplicity. James Boswell, biographer of Samuel Johnson, recorded how the latter, because he did not want his servant to lie, would retreat to the attic without mentioning it to his servant, so if anyone called, the servant could honestly say he didn't know where his master was. Johnson reasoned thus, "If I allow my servant to tell a lie for me, don't I have reason to expect that he will tell many lies himself?"

Lying sometimes convicts the wrong man. It helped crucify Christ and stone Stephen, for false witnesses were found at both trials. No one this side of the judgment can measure the damage done by the slandering tongue. "A tongue three inches long can kill a man six feet tall."

Ben Johnson said, "Slander cuts men's throats with whisperings." What fires it can start! What poison it can spread! He who slanders does the devil's work, for devil means slanderer: he is the accuser of the brethren. Dr. A. B. Simpson said, "I would rather play with forked lightning or take in my hands living wires, with their fiery currents, than speak a reckless word against any servant of Christ or idly repeat the slanderous darts which thousands of Christians are hurling on others."

Lying affects our relationship with God   Lying not only harms the one who lies and upsets society, but it also affects our relationship with God. Habitual lying may indicate we are not God's child but rather under the sway of Satan who "is a liar, and the father of lies" (John 8:44). Lying is contradictory to God's nature, for He is truth.

Lying unless forgiven, will keep us from heaven. After the glorious picture of the New Jerusalem (Rev. 21) comes a warning that into that city shall not enter "anything that defileth, neither whatsoever worketh abomination, or maketh a lie" (v. 27). Again in the last chapter of the Bible we are told, "For without are dogs, and sorcerers, and whoremongers, and murderers, and idolaters, and whosoever loveth and maketh a lie" (22:15).

A woman in Western Canada sent her child to Sunday School. He learned many things that differed from his mother's churchless way of life. At the railway ticket office, as they were about to take a trip east, she quietly told the boy to lie about his age, and thus save her $25 on the fare. But the boy unexpectedly blurted out, "No, Mom, I'm not going to hell for $25."

We must recognize the sinfulness of our lives, which helped nail Christ to the cross, and ask Him to forgive us through His redeeming sacrifice. Then as God's children, we'll have His indwelling Spirit to enable us to keep this New Testament command, "Wherefore putting away lying, speak every man truth with his neighbour" (Eph. 4:25). What good a dedicated tongue can do —evangelize, edify, teach, encourage, inform, inspire, comfort. John Bunyan claimed that the turning point in his life came one day when he chanced to overhear four poor women sitting at a doorway, talking about the new birth and all it meant to them, a conversation that went inescapably with him.

Don Landaas, a member of the elite Marine Ceremonial Guard, was on helicopter guard detail at Camp David in May 1959, the weekend President Eisenhower was entertaining England's Prime Minister Macmillan. Doing what he shouldn't have been, he slid back the door of Eisenhower's helicopter, sat down, and began to pray. Superior officers of the guard happened to be checking at that moment, caught him off his post, arrested him, and sent him back to the guardhouse in Washington for disciplinary action.

His buddies advised him to say he thought he had heard a noise in the helicopter and was investigating. But he prayed for strength to tell the truth at the court-martial.

On the day of the trial, Landaas stood before a colonel and 10 other officers. After the charges were read, the colonel asked Landaas if he had anything to say for himself.

Replied Landaas, "Colonel, I should like to tell the truth. That night at Camp David I didn't go into the helicopter because I heard anything. I went in there because I wanted to pray. As a

Christian I have dedicated myself to my Master just as you, a colonel in the Marine Corps, are a man dedicated to your commander."

The colonel replied, "Landaas, I believe you, but I have no alternative but to punish you. Had someone slipped up by the side of the helicopter when you were inside and poured water in the gas tank, you might have been responsible for the president's death."

Landaas was sentenced to 20 days hard labor, fined $50, and busted from first class to buck private. Said the colonel, "Your court-martial removes your top secret clearance so you can no longer guard the president." But because of his otherwise fine record, the imprisonment was suspended and he was given a choice of duties.

Two weeks later, Landaas, an accomplished accordion player, had an audition with the Marine Band, and was appointed accordion soloist for the last two years of his military hitch.

Comments Landaas, who in recent years has given musical performances in many churches and Bible conferences, "I saw that telling the truth is the only course for a Christian to follow. As a member of the Marine Band I started out as a sergeant. I sewed three stripes on the arm from which one had been removed two weeks before. Three months later, when Eisenhower returned to Camp David for his weekend talks with Khrushchev, I was one of six musicians chosen to go along to provide the music. I returned to Camp David, a place I had been told I would never set foot in again. I flew up in the same helicopters I had previously guarded, including the one I had prayed in and had been arrested in. I met President Eisenhower, spoke with him, played for him, and in the following months for 20 other heads of state. It pays to tell the truth."

11

Nip It in the Bud

Commandment Ten: "Thou shalt not covet" (Ex. 20:17).

When inflation accelerated in our economy in 1974, a bill collector reported an entirely new class of folks not paying their bills. He commented, "We are getting basically honest people who never had problems paying their bills before. These debtors haven't yet learned that inflation is cutting deeply into their life-style. They are used to going out to dinner, to the theater, and buying new clothes regularly. All of a sudden they haven't got enough to pay for everything, but they're not willing to cut down their mode of living. They don't want to go back to their lower life-style." In effect, these debtors craved too strongly their good way of life. They coveted their luxuries.

Covetousness is not confined to our decade. An unusual advertisement appeared in England in 1836, offering a prize of 100 guineas (roughly $500) to the author of the best essay on the sin of covetousness. The ad began, "Many of the wisest and best of men are of the opinion that there is no sin so prevalent among professors of the Gospel as the love of money, and yet there is no subject on which so little has been written well." The winning essay was titled *Covetousness: the Sin of the Christian Church*. It is now in book form, called *Mammon: The Demon of Greed* (John Harris, Bible Truth Depot, Swengel, Pa.).

The tenth commandment reads in full: "Thou shalt not covet thy neighbor's house; thou shalt not covet thy neighbor's wife, nor his manservant, nor his maidservant, nor his ox, nor his ass, nor anything that is thy neighbor's" (Ex. 20:17). These seven items are summarized in most listings of the Decalogue simply as "Thou shalt not covet" (see Rom. 13:9).

What Is Covetousness?

Without the instinct for acquisition we could not support ourselves nor our families and would become intolerable burdens on others. The Bible does not forbid setting things aside for the future. The sluggard is told to take a leaf from the provident ant who in summer gathers food for winter (Prov. 6:6-8). Paul warned, "If any provide not for his own, and specially for those of his own house, he hath denied the faith, and is worse than an infidel" (1 Tim. 5:8). But when the acquisitive instinct gets out of hand, it becomes just plain covetousness.

Excessive desire for what one doesn't have   Covetousness may be defined, in part, as "inordinate desire for what one does not have." Various words are translated *covet* or *covetousness*. For example, when Paul says, "I have coveted no man's silver" (Acts 20:33), the word means "the exercise of lust" or "overmastering desire." Coveting after money (1 Tim. 6:10) is literally "extending" (the arm) or "craving." Three times a compound is used which means "love of silver" or "money." But the most frequently used word is another compound which means "having more," implying greedy desire.

Years ago, the book *Keeping Up with Lizzie* told of a small town grocer's daughter who went to college, where the new environment created new desires in her. Months later the young lady returned home in the first automobile to be seen in that area. This novelty aroused such desire in the townfolk to get cars, that people went into debt, even mortgaging their homes to keep up with Lizzie.

A hungry desire to keep up with the Joneses is fed us by the mass media of our day. The average viewer is bombarded by about 90 commercials during his several hours per day before the TV set. He is further exposed to newspapers, magazines, billboards, third-class mail, and other sources. It is estimated that the typical American consumer sees or hears a total of around

1,600 advertisements every day. These stimulate the purchase of previously unknown or unwanted products, and encourage the increasing consumption of things to bring happiness or prove success. This insane, insatiable hankering after the goods, styles, and services of the contemporary world symptomizes the disease of greed. No matter how high the salary, some couples live from paycheck to paycheck.

Sister sins are the passion to get rich, to make a fast buck, avarice, hoarding, wastefulness, and extravagance.

Desire to have what belongs to another   When this greed is directed toward another's property, house, land, car, furniture, business, boat, wife, or whatever, it is covetousness. When full grown, this desire to have what one has no right to possess blossoms into willingness to use dishonorable means to secure it for oneself.

More recent versions of the Bible translate the King James *covetousness* as "bribe, unjust gain, ruthless greed, rapacity"; and *covetous* as "grabber" (see Ex. 18:21; Prov. 28:16; Mark 7:22; Rom. 1:29; 1 Cor. 5:10).

A fuller definition of covetousness would be "excessive desire for what one does not have, especially what belongs to another." A desire can be inordinate because of its excess, even though for a legitimate object. Or a desire may be inordinate because it is pointed at a neighbor's possession.

Importance of This Commandment

If asked which is the least important of the Ten Commandments, most would reply the tenth. Compared to theft, adultery, and murder, how unimposing it sounds.

A confessor who had heard many penitents said, "No one ever confessed covetousness."

A minister stated, "Among all the prayers in prayer meeting and deep confessions of sin in times of searching, I have never once heard the sin of covetousness acknowledged."

One preacher spoke on this vice under the subject "The Sin We Never Admit."

So universal, so hidden, so powerful, but so deceptive is this sin that we are scarcely aware of its existence. But a little reflection will show how critical and crucial this seemingly insignificant commandment is.

It penetrates to the heart. This command enters another world, the inner one, piercing beyond act to attitude. All other commandments forbid overt sin, but this one reaches to inner motives, condemning as evil the entertaining of the thoughts of wrong-doing. This indicates the divine origin of this commandment, for only God knows what goes on in the human mind and would thus be able to enforce it.

No human legislator, no earthly congress, no temporal king could effectively forbid covetousness. No police radar can detect wrong intent. Imagine a police officer in court trying to prove a man was *thinking* of running off with his neighbor's wife. But divine authority reaches to our very thought life. The secrets of all hearts are open before Him and bare before His eyes.

This commandment thus shows the impossibility of earning heaven by keeping the law. God demands not only faultless behavior, but a flawless thought life as well, which no one possesses. It was this sin which brought conviction to the Apostle Paul, who wrote, "I had not known sin, but by the law; for I had not known lust, except the law had said, 'Thou shalt not covet' " (Rom. 7:7). To merit heaven by keeping the law would require a heart that never had a covetous thought. But the Bible asserts that man's heart is deceitful above all things, and desperately wicked (Jer. 17:9). Though outward misdeeds lower us in the eyes of society, inward thoughts condemn us in the eyes of God.

It is pivotal. Far from a harmless, inconsequential rule, the tenth commandment is a key command, for it involves a sin which begets every other sin. It is a door which leads to the violation of all the other nine. Perhaps this is why covetousness is listed with the most flagrant of sins by biblical writers (Rom. 1:29-31; Mark 7:21-23; Eph. 5:3-5).

Commandments One and Two—These two commands require that we love God supremely. Coveting displaces God with some other object. When happiness of heart is sought in some other god, covetousness has become idolatry, which is what the New Testament calls it (Eph. 5:5; Col. 3:5).

Since money is the medium of exchange which permits the

purchase of whatever we covet, love of money is a close equivalent to covetousness. As mentioned earlier, one word appearing three times in the New Testament and translated *covetousness* means literally "love of silver [money]." Money-itis can be disastrous. Love of money kept the rich young ruler from Christ and eternal life. Love of money put the rich fool in hell. As a penny held close enough to the eye can blot out the sun, so money can eclipse the Sun of righteousness. Mammon madness makes men bow to the Almighty Dollar instead of to Almighty God, which violates the foremost of the commands.

Commandment Three (cursing)—Many a person, wanting something badly and blocked in his attempts to get it, has been known to release a string of violent oaths. Temporary or permanent thwarting of greed has so often led to blasphemy of God's holy name.

Commandment Four (Sabbath)—Nehemiah rebuked the Israelites in the days of the restoration for bringing goods into Jerusalem to sell on the Sabbath (Neh. 13:15-22). The merchants coveted greater profits.

A theater in a Pennsylvania city where Sunday movies were prohibited hung out a motto: "Go to church Sunday; attend movies during the week." But when a town referendum to permit Sunday movies was proposed, the theater scrapped its motto and worked hard for an affirmative vote. Sunday opening meant more shekels.

Commandment Five (parents)—Through legal quibble it was possible for a person of Jesus' day to avoid the responsibility of supporting his parents by dedicating his property to the temple. At the same time he was allowed to continue enjoying the proceeds himself. Jesus unmasked this covetous practice charging, "Why do ye also transgress the commandment of God by your tradition? For God commanded, saying, 'Honor thy father and mother'" (Matt. 15:3-4). In an eastern state, a young man was charged with hiring a gunman to kill his parents. His motive? He was the sole heir to a substantial legacy.

Commandment Six (killing)—Ahab's sulking greed for a particular vineyard resulted in the death of Naboth its owner (1 Kings 21:1-16).

Judas' fever for money not only led him to pilfer from the treasury bag, but finally to betray Jesus to certain death for a paltry 30 pieces of silver.

In our crime-ridden society robbers think nothing of senselessly killing their victims, even for minimal loot. Mammon can lead to murder.

Munitions makers have been charged with fomenting wars to make profits, even with selling arms to both sides in the same conflict. The real cause of many wars is the desire to improve economic status. Territorial aggrandizement, colonial expansion, and capture of areas with valuable resources like oil all stem from the desire for a higher standard of living. James asks, "Whence come wars and fightings among you? Come they not hence, even of your lusts that war in your members?" (4:1)

Not only murder, but all desecrations against another person's dignity, like oppression, violence, and injury are forbidden in this command. An underlying cause of social injustice in his day was declared by the Prophet Micah, "They covet fields, and take them by violence; and houses, and take them away; so they oppress a man and his house" (2:2). Greed made Felix keep Paul a prisoner when he would have released him for a few pieces of silver (Acts 24:26). James spoke of slave laborers whose wages had been withheld or reduced because of the greed of rich owners (5:4-5). Avarice caused slavery and all the misery that accompanied this blight. A drug pusher creates a dope addict to make money out of the victim's habit.

Commandment Seven (adultery)—Illicit sexual conduct begins with coveting. A person desires someone else's mate, setting the stage for the well-known triangle and adultery. David, idle at Jerusalem when he should have been in battle, saw Bathsheba, coveted her, committed adultery, then had her husband killed in battle (2 Sam. 11).

Covetousness can lead to family breakdowns. Love of money may make a man neglect his wife and family. Someone said, "Troubles in marriage often begin when a man becomes so busy earning his salt that he forgets his sugar." Or love of money may lead both husband and wife to extravagance and financial troubles. High on the list of causes of divorce is incompatibility, which often should be spelled *income-patability*. Many a gold digger has set her feather for a wealthy man, breaking up his marriage or leading him into a ridiculous alliance. Why do theater owners show pornographic movies? Simple—the love of money!

Commandment Eight (stealing)—Though taking booty from captured Jericho was divinely forbidden, Achan couldn't resist an expensive Babylonian garment, 200 shekels of silver, and a wedge of gold of 50 shekels weight. He confessed, "I coveted them" (Josh. 7:21). As a result, Israel was defeated at Ai with the loss of 36 lives, besides the exposure and death for Achan and his family.

People gamble because they covet easy money. Covetousness leads to shady business practices, like a dairyman diluting milk with water, or a grocer putting his best apples on top, or a student paying a ghost writer to prepare his term paper. Martin Luther threatened excommunication to a man who planned to sell a house for over 13 times what he had paid. Luther suggested a price less than half what the man was asking. Despite inflation in his time, Luther labeled this man's intended price exorbitant and unbridled covetousness.

Commandment Nine (lying)—Gehazi, Elisha's servant, pursued after Naaman, captain of the Syrian armies, whose gifts had been refused by Elisha. He pretended his master had changed his mind and was asking for a talent of silver and two changes of garments for himself.

God revealed the lie and the servant's greed to Elisha who pronounced the punishment of Naaman's leprosy on Gehazi and his family (2 Kings 5:15-27). "Ill-gotten gain brings ruin in its train."

The soldiers who guarded Jesus' tomb at the time of the resurrection were given hush money to report a lie, namely that His disciples stole His body at night when they were asleep. Ananias and Sapphira pretended to bring an offering of all the sale proceeds from their property, while through covetousness they were keeping some for themselves.

So breaking the tenth commandment may lead to the violation of one or more of the other nine. How much misery can be traced to failure to refrain from coveting. A resident of Springfield,

Ill. was drawn to the door one day by the crying of children. He saw Abraham Lincoln walking by with his two sons, both crying.

"What's the matter?" asked the neighbor.

Lincoln replied crisply, "Just what is the matter with the whole world. I have three walnuts and each boy wants two!" How much of our domestic, national, and international dissention springs from covetousness.

No wonder Jesus warned, "Beware of covetousness; for a man's life consisteth not in the abundance of the things which he possesseth" (Luke 12:15). To reinforce the warning, Jesus then related the parable of the rich fool, who through greed built bigger, more bulging barns, but who was poor toward heaven and unprepared when called suddenly into the presence of his Maker. Says a sober proverb, "He will never have enough till his mouth is filled with mold."

How to Cure Covetousness

1. Guard your heart.   Every crime was once a thought. If we never entertain an evil design, we'll not likely commit it. How carefully we should watch the springs of the heart from which the rivers of action flow. Condemn and check the first motions of the inner man toward any sinful desire. Harbor no lust of flesh, lust of eye, nor pride of life. Stifle the first bubbling of evil within. It's easier to kill a snake when it's still an egg, than when a huge, dangerously slithering, striking serpent. So, nip any covetous thought in the bud. Someone said, "When you're looking at your neighbor's melon patch, you may not be able to keep your mouth from watering, but you can run." Paul advised, in warning against the love of money as the root of all evil, "O man of God, flee these things" (1 Tim. 6:11). Or, as the writer of Proverbs put it, "Keep thy heart with all diligence, for out of it are the issues of life" (4:23).

2. Cultivate contentment.   Discontent spawns desire. Our high standard of living makes the luxuries of yesterday become the necessities of today. One man said, "Let us all be happy and live within our means, even if we have to borrow money to do it." But things do not satisfy. If happiness came through things (covetousness is based on this supposition), Americans should be the happiest people on earth. Yet our country has more people who are depressed and using pills than most other nations.

The antidote to covetousness is contentment. Epicurus said, "If you want to make a man happy, add not to his possessions, but take away from his desires." Our manner of life is to "be without covetousness" ("love of silver," Heb. 13:5). Paul said, "Godliness with contentment is great gain. For we brought nothing into this world, and it is certain we can carry nothing out. And having food and raiment let us be therewith content" (1 Tim. 6:6-8). We can learn from the frugal farmer, who visiting a new shopping center for the first time exclaimed, "I don't know when I've seen so many things I could do without."

Two brothers owned a successful business. They were offered a controlling interest in a new company which they could supervise. They refused thus: "We have families. We are also officers in our church. We make more than a comfortable living with time left over to give to family and church. If we take over this new company, it would mean long, long hours. We have decided that we cannot sacrifice our families, our health, and the Lord's work to make more money we really don't need."

3. Tithe. Someone advised, "If you wish to be delivered from the love of money, give freely." First, we should give our tithe to the Lord's work. Failure to tithe is robbing God (Mal. 3:8-9). Why do most people fail to tithe? Simply because they prize their money too highly. Tithing helps cut the nerve of selfishness, making us giving persons instead of grabbing ones. The death of covetousness comes through the birth of charity. One professional man, to curb excessive desire to increase his earning power, determined to give four times his usual percentage of contributions when he reached a certain income level.

4. Enjoy your possessions with moderation. When a Christian has tithed, even given generously beyond the tithe, and still has some money left over, is it right to use that surplus to buy some of the comforts of life for personal enjoyment? Paul seems to suggest that possibility. Even while warning the rich against pride and the uncertainty of riches, and reminding them to be rich in good works and to share, Paul urges them to trust "in the living *God, who giveth us richly all things to enjoy"* (1 Tim. 6:17).

How can a sincere Christian rightfully use his financial surplus for personal enjoyment, and at the same time show concern for the evangelization of the lost and the relief of the needy? Dr. Donald Lake, in a Wheaton (Ill.) College chapel address, suggested the principle of immaterialization, then illustrated it.

It involves two key concepts:

(1) it is spiritually permissible for the Christian to enjoy whatever economic surplus the Lord has given, provided the surplus was not received either as a violation of the laws of God or the laws of men; (2) all enjoyments must be matched by an equal gift to the work of Christ. . . . Suppose I desire to purchase a beautiful picture for a room in my home. If the picture costs $50, the principle of immaterialization requires that I match the $50 purchase with a $50 donation to the work of Christ. . . . If I cannot match my personal purchase for enjoyment's sake with an equal contribution to the work of Christ, then I cannot purchase the item for personal enjoyment (*God Speaks to an X-rated Society,* edited by Alan F. Johnson, Moody Press, Chicago).

Dr. Lake, who coined the phrase *principle of immaterialization,* says three additional principles are required for its practical outworking: (1) every Christian should have a regular program of giving; (2) he should make over and above gifts for special needs to which the Holy Spirit has brought strong sensitivity; (3) he should keep short accounts when luxury purchases are made, so that the matching gift is made immediately or settled on a monthly basis.

5. *Think often of the cross of Christ.* When a forest fire broke out in the Pyrenees Mountains, the heat so penetrated the ground that a stream of pure silver gushed out, revealing for the first time the existence of this rich metal. Covetousness hides and hoards, but the melting power of the cross, kindled in the heart, can release a believer's silver to flow in the service of the Lord.

A Christian woman, a faithful tither for many years, came to church early one Sunday morning with her heart set on buying some lovely clothes. When her husband's check had arrived Saturday, she had thought, *This one time I'll not put in the tithe. I'll give only $1, so I'll have money to purchase that dress.*

But that Sunday morning she was helping on the committee to prepare the elements for the communion table. As she started to fill the little glasses, the Lord began to speak to her about her plan to withhold the tithe to use for her own self. Examining herself, she cried out, "O Lord, I cannot take the Lord's Supper till I know You are pleased with me."

She solemnly promised God that when she cashed that check, she would give the tithe to Him. Later in the service, in sweet peace and remembrance of the One who sacrificed all for us, she partook of the elements which pictured His broken body and shed blood. The hymn writer put it this way:

> *See from His head, His hands, His feet,*
> *Sorrow and love flow mingled down;*
> *Did e'er such love and sorrow meet,*
> *Or thorns compose so rich a crown?*
>
> *Were the whole realm of nature mine,*
> *That were a present far too small;*
> *Love so amazing, so divine,*
> *Demands my soul, my life, my all.*

12

The Law and the Lamb

"Christ hath redeemed us from the curse of the law,
being made a curse for us" (Gal. 3:13).

A waitress in a hotel housing a denomination's annual convention was heard to remark, "These people came with $10 bills and the Ten Commandments—and they haven't broken any of them."

Though church folks might be tight with their tips, it could never be said that anyone, even religious folks, had ever completely kept the Ten Commandments. Every last person on earth, the moral as well as the most vile, has failed to keep the law of God perfectly.

All Have Broken the Ten Commandments

James, a good man who had never harmed anyone, was the chauffeur for a fine Christian businessman. Many times the employer tried to tell James that he needed the Saviour, but whenever he did so, the standard reply was, "I keep the Ten Commandments. What more do I need?"

One day the employer said to James, "If you can keep God's Law for half an hour, I'll give you that Buick of mine that you like to drive around when you don't have to use the Cadillac."

"Oh, thank you, sir," James said excitedly. "That's so good of you. I do like that Buick. I can easily keep the Ten Commandments for half an hour, for I always keep them."

His employer told him to go up to the rumpus room over the garage, and lock the door to keep out noise and to lessen temptation. The half hour soon passed. Down came James, saying, "I certainly want to thank you for the Buick."

But his employer asked, "What did you do while you were up in the rumpus room?"

"Oh, I was just thinking."

"And what were you thinking?" asked the businessman.

"Why, to tell the truth, sir," said the chauffeur, "I was just thinking that since you're so good as to give me the Buick, maybe you'd let me have that set of extra new tires in the garage, because the tires are not good on that Buick."

"Oh, James," replied the employer, "I'm sorry to say that I cannot give you even the Buick. The Law says, 'Thou shalt not covet!' and you were coveting while up in that rumpus room. You haven't kept the Ten Commandments even half an hour, much less all your life!"

The Law reaches into the thought life. Unlike any set of human laws, the divinely given Decalogue penetrates to our thought life. No earthly sovereign could enforce a law that pertains to our thinking, for no mortal can read another's mind. How could a traffic policeman prove that a motorist was thinking of breaking a 50-mile-an-hour speed limit? But God who knows our thoughts afar off can extend and enforce His laws to the innermost recesses of our mind.

The Law stimulates rebellion in the sinful heart. Strange as it may seem, the Law stirs up the lawlessness of the human heart. When the manager of a seaside hotel discovered a broken window, caused by a heavy sinker on a fishing line blown back by the stiff breeze, he put a notice in every room that fishing off the balconies was prohibited. Soon several windows were broken in a similar manner. So the management removed all notices forbidding balcony fishing. No more windows were broken. The law against such fishing had aroused the sinful propensities of many hotel guests.

Commandments often bring out the evil within us. That's why Paul wrote, "I had not known sin, but by the law. . . . But sin, taking occasion by the commandment, wrought in me all manner of concupiscence. . . . But when the commandment came, sin revived" (Rom. 7:7-9). Unlike every other ancient code of morality, the Decalogue is formulated in short, imperative, negative clauses. This seems to indicate that they are addressed to those who possess an evil heart in a state of rebellion against God. A newspaper printed the Ten Commandments without giving their source. An indignant reader wrote, "You are becoming too personal. Cancel my subscription."

The Law demands love to God. Many think that somehow fulfilling obligations to fellowmen is sufficient. But the Decalogue divides into two sections: love to God (first four commandments), and love to man (last six). Even if we were 100% faithful in our duty to our neighbor (which we are not), we would still need to have perfect love toward God. But no one has ever loved God completely with never a lapse of devotion. Who can say, "As the heart panteth after the water brooks, so panteth my soul after Thee, O God"? (Ps. 42:1) If you don't thirst after Him with that fervor, then you have not kept the Decalogue. If we don't love God with our whole heart, soul, and mind, we have failed in keeping the first and great commandment (Matt. 22:37-38).

Dale Evans in *My Spiritual Diary* admits, "As much as it hurts me to face it, I must: early this morning, driving across Laurel Canyon and thinking over the years that are gone, I realized suddenly that there isn't one of God's commandments that I haven't broken, in one way or another—either by act, thought, or the spoken word. That's a pretty terrible record" (Revell, Old Tappan, N.J.). As the psalmist said, "If Thou, Lord, shouldest mark iniquities, O Lord, who shall stand?" (Ps. 130:3) No wonder Martin Luther found his attempts to find peace through the law futile.

All Are under the Penalty of a Broken Law

How often the law-breaker in the Old Testament was to be put to physical death—for cursing the Lord's name (Lev. 24:10-16), for killing a person (24:17), for breaking the Sabbath (Num. 15:32-36). But sin, which has been defined as lawlessness (the want of conformity to the law of God), brings eternal death. "The wages of sin is death" (Rom. 6:23).

To break one is to be guilty of all. Some take refuge in claiming, "I've broken only one of the commandments, so I'm really not so bad after all." But the Bible says, "Whosoever shall keep the whole law, and yet offend in one point, he is guilty of all" (James 2:10).

This does not mean that if a person breaks one law he may as well go ahead and break the others. Nor does it mean that one sin is as bad as another, for murder certainly is worse than coveting. But it does mean that the offender who breaks the law at just one point is just as guilty as the person who breaks all the commands. To violate just one rule displays a spirit of disobedience to the divine will and brings the same penalty as if one had broken all the commands.

All men are equally sinners, though all haven't sinned equally. Men are equal in the fact of law-breaking, though not the degree of law-breaking. Conversation like this is not likely to be heard behind prison bars, "You're a worse fellow than I. I only snatched a purse, but you robbed a bank." Though one may have committed a worse crime, both are law-breakers and both must pay penalties.

The ten links form a unity.　　God's law constitutes a grand and glorious unity. If your jet from New York to Hawaii takes 10 hours, and for the first nine flies smoothly, but during the tenth crashes into the Pacific, you're still in trouble.

A heavy chandelier, held up by a thick chain of 10 strong links, hangs over your head in a spacious, ornate, and crowded dining hall. If just one link breaks, think of the damage and possible deaths.

A tight-rope walker with no net beneath him has 10 yards left to make it safely across. For nine yards there's not a misstep, but on the last yard, he misses the rope and falls.

No matter where you step onto a lawn bearing a "no trespassing" sign, you become a trespasser. You cannot say, "Oh, I just trespassed in one spot so I'm not a very big trespasser."

He who violates one divine law cannot hide behind the idea that he has merely broken a rule which is isolated from the general law of God. Rather he is guilty of a breach of the law which takes in all commandments, thus placing himself in rebellion against God as though he had broken all rules.

One broken law is enough to condemn.　　So many feel that

at the judgment their good deeds will be weighed against their evil deeds. More good ones mean heaven; more evil ones mean hell. But it won't be that way. No man guilty of robbing a bank ever pleads, "Judge, think of the thousands of banks I never robbed. I only robbed one. I should go free." Nor does a convicted murderer beg clemency, "I only murdered one man. There are 200 million people in this country I never killed." A man is tried for the crime he commits, regardless of the ones he never committed. Every member of the human race is guilty of specific violations of God's law, which, if unforgiven, will send him to a lost eternity.

If we are honest, we would have to admit that we have countless transgressions charged against us. A man who claimed he didn't sin much admitted to one transgression a day. He was reminded that this would figure out to 365 a year, and in ten years, over 3,650. Since he had lived 50 years since his teens, he had over 18,000 sins to answer for.

He who tries to gain heaven by keeping the law puts himself under a curse. Paul wrote, "Cursed is everyone that continueth not in all things which are written in the book of the law to do them" (Gal. 3:10). Unless one continues to keep every law all the time, with never an exception, he is under the penalty of a broken law. That's why Paul began this section, "As many as are of the works of the law [trying to gain heaven through keeping the law] are under the curse."

Since every member of the human race has broken the Decalogue, all are doomed, unless God provides a way out. And that He has already done through His Son, the Lord Jesus Christ, the Lamb of God.

Christ Bore the Curse of a Broken Law

How significant that when God gave Moses the Ten Commandments from Mt. Sinai, He also gave the details for the construction of the tabernacle and for its sacrificial system. Sacrifices were to be offered daily as a prefigurement of how the breaking of the law could be forgiven. Along with the law God gave the lamb. A trail of broken laws could be forgiven only by a trail of blood. The high point in the tabernacle ritual was the Day of Atonement, when the blood of a sacrificed goat was sprinkled over the broken tables of the law in the Holy of Holies, and a live goat was released into the wilderness on whom the high priest had laid his hands in confession of the people's sins (Lev. 16).

In the Old Testament sacrificial system, the innocent animal gave its life for the guilty law-breaker, foreshadowing the Lamb of God who would lay down His life to take away the sins of the world (John 1:29). Christ declared that He came to give His life a ransom for many (Matt. 20:28), and that His blood would be "shed for many for the remission of sins" (Matt. 26:28). Peter wrote that Christ "His own self bare our sins in His own body on the tree" (1 Peter 2:24), and that He "hath once suffered for sins, the just for the unjust, that He might bring us to God" (3:18). The death of Christ was substitutionary; it was in our place.

Explicitly referring to the Ten Commandments, Paul declared that "Christ hath redeemed us from the curse of the law, being made a curse for us" (Gal. 3:13); also that Christ was "made under the law, to redeem them that were under the law, that we might receive the adoption of sons" (4:4-5). Becoming a member of the human race through the incarnation, Jesus Christ was placed under obligation to keep the Ten Commandments. Alone, of all humanity, He kept them perfectly. Thus He had no transgressions for which He had to pay the penalty. When He suffered, it was for the sins of others. He took the curse of a broken law that we might not only be forgiven, but also restored to full-fledged sonship in the divine family.

A man was heard to say that it took him 14 years to find out something very important. Asked what it was, he replied, "I found out that, one, I could not do anything for my salvation, two, that God didn't require me to do one thing, and three, that God had done it all through His Son's sacrifice." The Gospel is the Good News that follows the bad news. The bad news is that our sins leave us guilty before God and headed for a lost eternity. But the Good News is that "Christ died for our sins" (1 Cor. 15:3), so that when we acknowledge Him as our Saviour, no penalty hangs over our heads. He who deserved life received death in order that we who deserved death might receive life. The poet has written:

Upon a life I did not live,
Upon a death I did not die,
Another's life, another's death,
I stake my whole eternity.

A century ago, in a western state, a one-room rural school had a difficult time in securing a teacher. Its previous male teacher had been attacked by some of the bigger boys. But in September a new teacher appeared. When the boys saw him, they smiled. "He's not very big or strong. We'll show him a thing or two," they said.

The new teacher was short, wore glasses, and brought his own son to school as a member of the class. On the first day the teacher said, "Fellows, I think we ought to have some rules in our school, but I would like you to make them; also the penalty for breaking them." The boys were impressed by this suggestion. Lack of fairness by previous teachers had been a major cause of the trouble.

The boys began to suggest rules. Finally, 10 rules were written on the board. One read, "No one shall steal a lunch." The penalty beside it stated, "Five lashes on the back after the jacket has been removed." Since the boys came from a distance and could not go home at noon, to have your lunch stolen was a hardship on these growing, hungry guys.

All went well for a few weeks. Then one noon a lunch was missing. Another day, another lunch was stolen. Finally the teacher caught the culprit. When the class assembled after noon recess, the teacher seemed reluctant to reveal the identity of the thief. After some hesitation, he announced, "It's Willie."

Willie was the smallest boy in the class, thin and under-nourished. Everyone knew his folks were poor, so poor they didn't have enough food in their cabin to give him lunch every day. So, hungry little Willie stole the lunches.

As the teacher stood there, both he and the class wished there was a way out of the dilemma. But the law had been broken and the penalty had to be paid. So the teacher called Willie forward, and told him to remove his jacket. Whimpering, Willie began to un-pin it. He got one arm out. As he withdrew the other arm, a gasp went up from the class. He wore no undershirt; his back was bare. Because it was fall, it was assumed every boy would have an undershirt.

Willie's family was so poor they could not provide him with either sufficient food or proper clothing. How could he stand five lashes? The rule had been made on the assumption that an undershirt would absorb some of the lash's sting. Otherwise, the whipping might have serious effects.

The teacher lifted the whip, arm extended, ready to bring the lash down on this bare, emaciated, little back with its ribs protruding.

Suddenly a hand shot up. It was the teacher's son, who asked, "If someone went up and took Willie's place, and took his five lashes, could Willie go free?"

A smile slowly spread over the teacher's face. Gently he lowered the whip. "Yes," he replied, "if someone will come up front and offer to take Willie's place, and Willie says yes, Willie will go free."

Immediately, the teacher's son walked to the front. "Willie, may I take your place?"

Willie gratefully whimpered a yes, put on his jacket and went to his seat. The teacher's son removed his jacket, revealing the usual undershirt. Then the teacher whipped his own son who had done nothing wrong, while Willie, the guilty boy, went scot-free.

The God of heaven has 10 rules, commonly called "The Ten Commandments." He also has declared the penalty of eternal death for all who break any rule. Who has not broken, not just one, but many or all of the Commandments, not just once but countless times? But one day God's Son said to his Father, "May I go down and take their place?"

Father and Son agreed on the plan for man's redemption. On the cross God whipped His own Son, not for any sin He had done, for He was sinless, but for mankind's violations. The law had been broken and the penalty had to be paid. Just as little Willie had to say yes to the teacher's son, so we must say yes to God's Son. Isaiah prophesied of the coming Saviour, "He was wounded for our transgressions . . . the Lord hath laid on Him the iniquity of us all" (53:5-6).

The Law Expresses the Will of God for the Believer

Though the believer is no longer under the awful penalty of the law, nor under the law as a means of justification before God, the law is still an expression of God's will for our lives. The Ten Commandments inscribe God's laws in propositional form as a fixed rule of life, grounded ultimately in the nature of God. The moral law contained in the Decalogue (not the ceremonial nor the civil laws of Israel) provides a revelation of God's requirements for His creatures.

By nature man rebels against these laws. But at conversion, the transformation of his moral base cuts his rebellion and turns him in the direction of obedience. Through regeneration God puts His laws into the believer's mind and writes them in his heart (Heb. 8:10).

A girl sent to a boarding school was handed a copy of the rules. At one glance she knew she could never keep such intolerable regulations. At dinner that evening she was introduced to the headmistress. *What a lovely lady,* she thought. Next day her admiration grew. Soon she became one of the headmistress' most devoted followers.

Where were the nasty, irksome, restricting rules now? Her own desire was to please the headmistress. Love made the fulfillment of the law so much easier. Similarly, the impossible, curse-bringing regulations of the Decalogue can become a desirable, blessing-yielding way of life through love placed in the heart by the regenerating, indwelling Holy Spirit. A verse in an old hymnbook states:

> *Run, John, and live, the Law commands,*
> *But gives me neither legs nor hands;*
> *Yet better news the Gospel brings,*
> *It bids me fly, and gives me wings.*

A longtime deacon, rather difficult to get along with at times, told the pastor he was going to visit the Bible lands. "And when I get there, I'm going to climb Mt. Sinai and shout the Ten Commandments at the top of my lungs!"

"I've a better suggestion," the discerning pastor replied. "Stay at home and keep them."